Information Systems Er

Application Partitioning and Integration with SSADM

LONDON: HMSO

© **Crown copyright 1994**

Applications for reproduction should be made to HMSO

First published 1994

ISBN: 0 11 330622 9

For further information regarding CCTA products please contact:

CCTA Library
Rosebery Court
St Andrews Business Park
Norwich
NR7 0HS
01603-704704

Foreword

The **Information Systems Engineering Library** provides guidance on managing and carrying out Information Systems Engineering activities. In the IS lifecycle, Information Systems Engineering takes place once the IS strategy has been defined. It is concerned with the development and ongoing improvement of information systems up to the operational stage, and their maintenance whilst in operational use.

The Information Systems Engineering Library complements other CCTA products, in particular the project management method, PRINCE, and the systems analysis and design method, SSADM.

Volumes in the Information Systems Engineering Library are of interest to varying levels of staff from IS directors to IS providers, helping them to improve the quality and productivity of their IS development work. Some volumes in this library should also be of interest to business managers, IS users and those involved in market testing, whose business operations depend on having effective IS support by means of Information Systems Engineering activities.

The Information Systems Engineering Library also complements other related CCTA publications, particularly the Programme and Project Management Library, the Information Management Library for data management issues, the IT Infrastructure Library for operational issues and the IS Planning Subject Guides for strategic issues.

CCTA welcomes customer views on Information Systems Engineering Library publications. Please send your comments to:

Information Systems Engineering Group
CCTA
Rosebery Court
St. Andrews Business Park
Norwich
NR7 0HS

Acknowledgements

CCTA gratefully acknowledges the help of the following organisation in the preparation of this volume:

Model Systems

Valuable review comments were provided by:

Inland Revenue
The Business Development Service of the
    Northern Ireland Civil Service
MoD
Kingston University
Pantechnology Ltd.

Contents

Chapter		page
Foreword		3
Acknowledgements		4
Contents		5
1	Introduction	7
	1.1 Purpose of this volume	7
	1.2 Who should read this volume	7
	1.3 Structure of this volume	8
	1.4 Overview of approach	10
	1.5 Introduction to example	15
2	3-schema Specification Architecture	21
	2.1 The SSADM Rationale	21
	2.2 The IT system is a simulation of the business	21
	2.3 A Conceptual Schema for information support	24
	2.4 A 3-schema Specification Architecture	27
	2.5 3-schema Specification Architecture and the SSADM Universal Function Model	29
3	Aspects	31
	3.1 'Aspect' as a view of an entity	31
	3.2 Corporate entities and project aspects	33
	3.3 Project partitioning	34
	3.4 Different behaviours (parallel lives)	37
	3.5 What is an aspect?	38
	3.6 Aspects and inheritance	39
4	Partitioning the Conceptual Model	43
	4.1 Summary of approach	43
	4.2 Identification of separately isolable areas of a data model	44
	4.3 Using aspects to decompose and isolate areas of a data model	47
	4.4 Developing enquiry views	52
	4.5 Developing entity life histories	59
	4.6 Aspects identified in analysis of parallel life histories	62

5		Integrating separately-developed Conceptual Models	65
	5.1	Summary	65
	5.2	Event processes within a single application	66
	5.3	Read-only access across applications	67
	5.4	Event processes spanning more than one application	70
	5.5	Ambiguous correspondences	74
	5.6	Reusable update processes	85
	5.7	Implementation of Conceptual Models	87
6		External Design	89
	6.1	Summary	89
	6.2	User roles	89
	6.3	Functions in the 3-schema Specification Architecture	90
	6.4	External Design of the first application	91
	6.5	External Design of subsequent applications	95
7		Internal Design	101
	7.1	Summary	101
	7.2	First-cut Internal Design	101
	7.3	Design optimisation	102
8		Issues	105
	8.1	Introduction	105
	8.2	There may be more than one way to partition applications	105
	8.3	Shared servers may be merged into applications	106
	8.4	Applications may get out of step	109
9		Impact on SSADM Structural Model	115
	9.1	Summary	115
	9.2	Business Activity Model	118
	9.3	Business Activity Model and Conceptual Model	119
	9.4	Current and Required Data Flow Models	120
	9.5	Changes to SSADM V4 Techniques	123
	9.6	SSADM Structural Model	126

Bibliography 139

Glossary 141

Index 151

1 Introduction

1.1 Purpose of this volume

The purpose of this volume is to provide guidance on:

- decomposition of large systems into smaller systems for separate development

- integration of closely-related but separately-developed systems.

The guidance is presented mainly at a technical level, as an extension of SSADM. It is applicable whether development is managed as sub-projects within a single overall project, or as separate projects within a programme.

Reasons for partitioning

There are three major reasons for partitioning a project for separate development and subsequent integration:

- incremental delivery

- parallel development of subsystems; this is often done for faster delivery, but may be needed to break a large and complex application area into simpler parts

- development of coordinated systems to serve different types of location in a distributed organisation.

The same general principles apply to all three types of development. In this volume we describe integration from the view of incremental delivery, and comment on the differences in approach for the other two.

1.2 Who should read this volume

The primary intended audience of this volume is experienced SSADM practitioners and team leaders.

The guidance should also be of interest to project managers and programme managers who are concerned with IS development, for whom the overview of the approach and the chapters on the 3-schema Specification Architecture and entity aspects will probably be of value.

Project managers will also find the final chapters which describe the impact on SSADM useful.

Readers' backgrounds

Readers should be familiar with SSADM Version 4 structure, products and terminology.

Those who wish to practise the approach should be experienced practitioners of SSADM, who have a good grounding in data modelling and entity-event modelling.

Related guidance

This volume builds on the ideas presented in *ISE Library Volume: Customising SSADM*. It is complemented by several other CCTA guides:

- *Distributed Systems: Application Development (ISE Library)*

- *Reuse in SSADM using OO (ISE Library)*

- *Corporate Data Modelling (Information Management Library)*.

In addition, some related ideas may be found in:

- *An Introduction to Reuse (ISE Library)*

- *Managing Reuse (ISE Library)*

- *Data Management (Information Management Library)*

- *An Introduction to Programme Management (Programme and Project Management Library)*

- *A Guide to Programme Management (Programme and Project Management Library)*.

1.3 Structure of this volume

This volume has a four part structure:

- introduction and overview of approach (this chapter)

Chapter 1
Introduction

- concepts underlying the approach (Chapters 2 and 3)
- detail of approach (Chapters 4 to 7)
- impact of approach on SSADM (Chapters 8 and 9).

Who should read which chapters	This chapter should be sufficient for readers who require an overview of the approach.

Experienced SSADM practitioners, team leaders and anyone interested in the concepts behind the approach should read Chapters 2 and 3.

Chapters 4 to 7 describe the technical detail of the approach and are aimed at experienced SSADM practitioners and team leaders.

Project managers should read, at least, this Chapter and Chapters 8 and 9. |
| Introduction and overview of approach | Section 1.4 provides an overview of the approach to application partitioning and integration with SSADM.

Section 1.5 introduces the 'Projects-R-Us' example, used throughout this volume to illustrate concepts, techniques and work products. |
| Concepts underlying the approach | The two major concepts used in the approach are described briefly in Section 1.4, and fully in:

- Chapter 2: 3-schema Specification Architecture
- Chapter 3: Entity aspects. |
| Detail of approach | The technical detail of the approach is described in terms of SSADM products and techniques, and illustrated with examples drawn from Projects-R-Us in:

- Chapter 4: Partitioning the Conceptual Model |

9

- Chapter 5: Integrating separately-developed Conceptual Models

- Chapter 6: External Design

- Chapter 7: Internal Design.

Impact of approach on SSADM	Chapter 8, Issues, identifies some limitations of the approach and some areas in which feedback from practical experience is needed.

Chapter 9, Impact on the SSADM Structural Model, describes the differences between the approach described in this volume and the default structural model in the *SSADM V4 Reference Manuals*.

1.4 Overview of approach

The approach has two underlying concepts:

- the partitioning of a business area's activities (in order to develop separate applications for each partition) and the subsequent integration of the separate applications are defined in terms of the Conceptual Model in the 3-schema Specification Architecture. (The effects of this partitioning on techniques for External and Internal Design are comparatively minor)

- the points of separation and integration are 'aspects' (application-oriented views) of real-world entities shared by the applications.

A technical procedure has been built on these concepts, using modified versions of SSADM Version 4 techniques and products. See Chapters 4 to 7. This procedure can be used within a structural model derived from the SSADM Version 4 default structural model. See Chapter 9.

1.4.1 3-schema Specification Architecture

The *ISE Library Volume: Customising SSADM* describes a 3-schema Specification Architecture for the specification and design of IT systems. The three schemata are:

- the Conceptual Model, which specifies the logical data model for the IT system, the processes needed to keep it up-to-date and extract information from it, and the corresponding inputs and outputs. The Conceptual Model is closely related to the business activity to be supported, regardless of how the IT services are organised and implemented

- the External Design, which specifies how processes in the Conceptual Model will be packaged into functions to serve tasks carried out in user roles; functions will be implemented as dialogues, menus and batch transactions. The External Design also specifies how functions will be implemented with a specific input-output technology

- the Internal Design, which specifies how the logical data model will be implemented as a database in a specific data storage technology, and how processes in the Conceptual Model will access stored data.

All three schemata are explicitly implemented as code. For example, dialogues implemented in Motif could invoke database updates and enquiries coded in C that use SQL2 to access data in a relational database.

Partitioning & integration

We specify application partitioning and integration mainly in terms of the Conceptual Model. Most of the differences from the SSADM V4 default approach are concerned with defining and managing the Conceptual Model.

1.4.2 Entity aspects

Some real-world entities need to be modelled in more than one application. We use the term 'aspect' for the representation of an entity type in a single application. For example, in the Projects-R-Us system described Section 1.5, there is an employee aspect in the project control application and another in the training management application.

The concept of 'aspect' is more than an entity-attribute definition in a logical data model. It also incorporates the behaviour to be modelled - its entity life history and the enquiries to which it contributes. In fact, the behaviour is the aspect's defining characteristic ('what do employees do in projects and how shall we support and manage their activities?') and the attributes follow from that.

Aspects & subtypes

In a sense, defining entity aspects is the opposite of defining entity sub- and supertypes. With sub- and supertypes we identify similar behaviour of different real-world entities. For example, project workers could be employees or contractors. Every project worker would be either an employee or a contractor. We would want to model the 'project worker' behaviour of employees and contractors in the same application.

With aspects we identify different behaviours of the same real-world entity. For example, an employee can work on projects and participate in a training scheme - ie can simultaneously be a projects-employee and a training-employee. We can model these two kinds of real-world behaviour in different applications.

Coordination of behaviour

Aspects in different applications usually need to be coordinated; there are two possibilities. First, there are often shared characteristics. For example, project control and training management applications both need employee name and department, to be able to send outputs to the employee. Secondly, what has happened in one application may constrain what can be done in another. For example, when defining an employee's assignments, the project control application will need to ask the training management application for the dates of courses scheduled for the employee.

Basis of approach

The development approach is based on creating a separate Conceptual Model for each application. Any real-world entity that appears in more than one application is modelled as an aspect in each. Integration of applications is then mainly concerned with coordinating the behaviour of different aspects of the same real-world entities.

One consequence of this approach is that each application is self-contained. Internal consistency is tested separately from coordination with other applications. Any application might, in the short term, be run independently (with suitable stop-gap measures to overcome problems of incomplete functionality).

1.4.3 Technical steps

The approach consists of five activities:

- partition the business area into applications
- develop a separate Conceptual Model for each application
- integrate the Conceptual Models
- develop the External Design
- develop the Internal Design.

Partitioning

Our starting point is a business area with an IS requirement that can be decomposed into a number of separate applications. The application areas may be given. If not, guidelines provided in Chapter 4 may be used.

We need an overview logical data model for the business area. This might have been developed as part of an IS strategy, it might be extracted from a corporate data model or we might have to develop it specifically. This data model is partitioned to correspond with the applications. Entities that appear in more than one application are represented by an aspect in each corresponding data model partition.

Separate Conceptual Models

For each application, we build a Conceptual Model from its partition of the overall logical data model. This means identifying attributes and developing process models, inputs and outputs for events and enquiries.

The procedure is generally similar to that for developing the Conceptual Model of a freestanding application.

Event and enquiry names are kept consistent across all applications. See Chapter 4, Partitioning the Conceptual Model.

Integration

Update and enquiry processes in an application's Conceptual Model are invoked by the External Design. Some updates and enquiries are not affected by integration - they are wholly contained within one application.

Some update and enquiry processes span more than one application. For each of these, the External Design invokes a 'home' application, which then invokes other connected applications. The connections between applications are always simple one-to-one communication between aspects of the same entity. See Chapter 5, Integrating separately-developed Conceptual Models.

There are several different implementation techniques, including subroutine calls, linkage of separately-compiled modules and client/server calls. Communication between applications may be local or remote.

External Design

In many cases, there will be no need to integrate External Designs. The guidelines for application partitioning may lead to distinct groups of users for each application.

Where services from multiple applications have to be provided to the same user, integration requires two kinds of change:

- adding new functions to a user's menu

- extending the scope of existing functions to allow them to invoke updates and enquiries in the new application. This often requires careful design of input-output formats to ensure that they are sufficiently flexible to accommodate addition of new updates and enquiries.

See Chapter 6, External Design.

Internal Design

Internal Design - design of the physical database and the program-data interface - differs only slightly from the standard SSADM approach. There is some additional guidance on whether to integrate databases for separate applications, or to keep them separate. In either case, the applications operate as if they each had their own database; integration is hidden in the program-data interface.

See Chapter 7, Internal Design.

1.5 Introduction to example

In subsequent chapters, concepts, techniques and products are illustrated using an example system - a project control and employee training system for the Projects-R-Us company.

1.5.1 Projects-R-Us business activity

Projects-R-Us undertakes time-and-materials projects for its clients. Projects are broken down into tasks, which are done by employees. An employee may be assigned to several tasks concurrently. A task may have at most one employee assigned to it at any given time; the assigned employee may be changed during the life of the task.

Projects-R-Us also runs training schemes, each containing several courses. An employee may be in at most one training scheme at a time. Usually a scheme member will attend one presentation of each course in the scheme.

The company is organised in departments; for example, research, product specification, technical writing. Each employee is employed by one department, and may change departments during his or her employment.

1.5.2 Information support needed for business activity

Information support is needed for project control and employee training; the required information can be represented in a data model. Some of the inputs are provided by sections other than project control and training management.

Project control	The project control section receives a specification for each new project, broken down into tasks, each with a start date, end date and man-day budget. Staff in the section have three major activities:

- assigning employees to tasks. For this they need to know the availability of employees in departments

- informing the accounts section what should be billed to clients. For this they need to know which tasks have been completed and how much time was spent on them.

- rescheduling and recalculating the budget for tasks during the life of a project. For this they need to know, on any given date, how much time has been spent on a task as a proportion of its budget, and what proportion of its elapsed time has passed.

They also have to deal with exceptions such as project cancellation before completion, or having to replace an employee on a task because they have resigned or are needed urgently for some other task.

Employee training	The training section receives a specification for each training scheme, describing the courses in the scheme. Staff in the section have to ensure that employees in schemes attend courses. For this they need to know who is in each scheme and when courses in each scheme are to be presented.

Employees are assigned to schemes and removed from schemes by the personnel section.

The training section has to provide administrative support by:

- sending joining instructions to employees about to attend course presentations. For this they need to know where a presentation is to be held, and where to send the joining instructions (employee's department)

- cancelling course presentations that have no bookings. For this they need to know, one week before a presentation is due to start, how many places have been booked

- letting employees know what grades they have received on courses they have attended; arranging attendance on a subsequent presentation of the same course for an employee who has not received an acceptable grade.

They also have to deal with exceptions such as employee resignation when part-way through a training scheme, scheme cancellation, withdrawal of course from scheme.

The Logical Data Model (LDM) for Projects-R-Us is shown at Figure 1.1. The LDM has been extracted from a corporate data model; many of the attributes are already known and are shown in Figure 1.1.

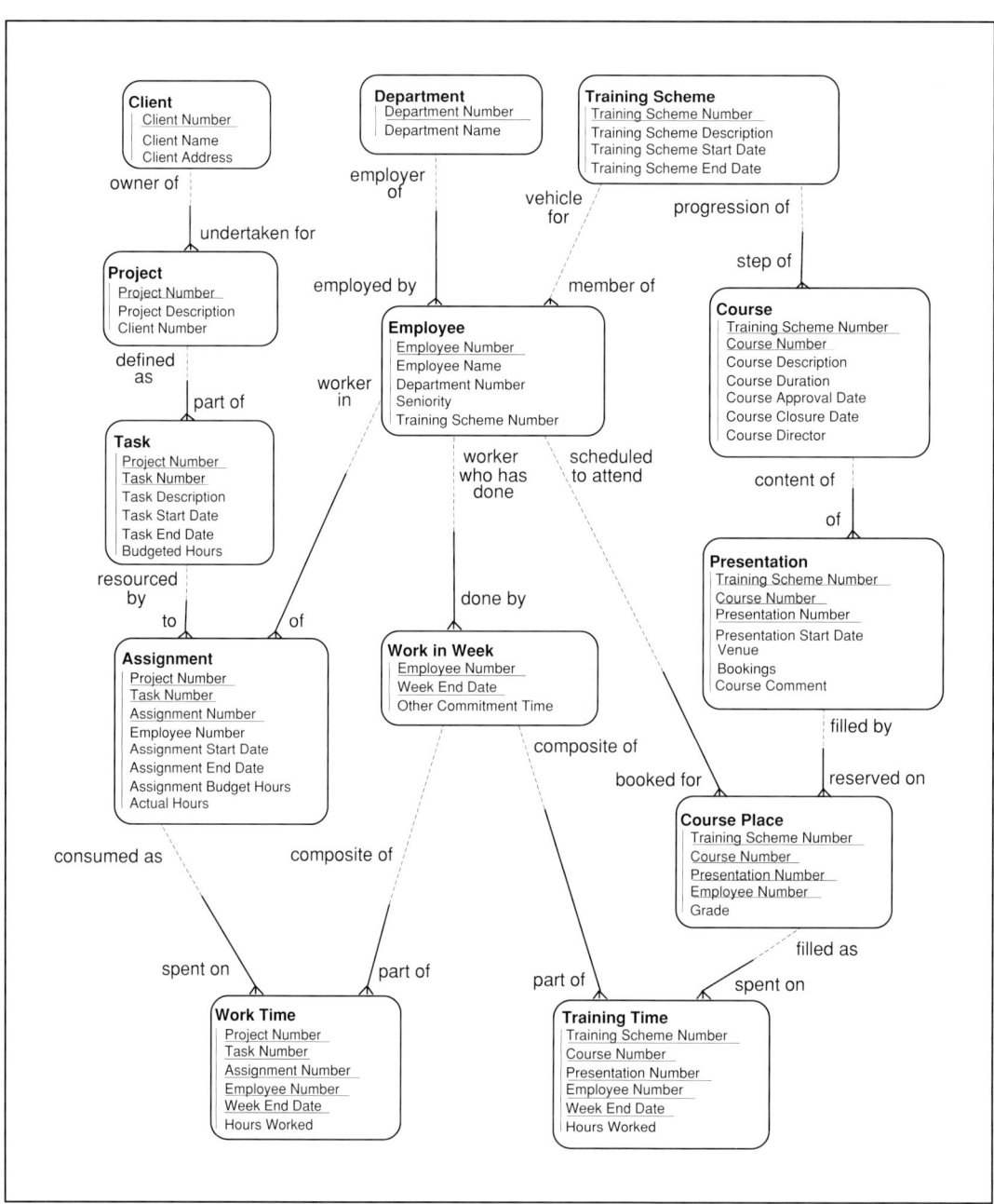

Figure 1.1: Logical Data Model for Projects-R-Us

1.5.3 Input needed to keep the LDM up-to-date

Project control — Project control staff create and terminate clients, projects, tasks and assignments in the LDM; they also set start and end dates and man-day budgets for tasks.

Training — Training section staff create and terminate training schemes and courses in LDM; they also input course presentations when they are notified, and create course places for employees.

At the end of a course presentation, training section staff record the grade for each employee who attended.

Personnel section — The personnel section supports project control and training by maintaining employee data. Both project and training sections need to know about employees and which departments they are in.

Personnel section staff create departments. They recruit employees and allocate them to departments, switch them between departments and deal with resignations.

Personnel staff also allocate employees to, and remove them from, training schemes.

Time recording — The time recording section supports project control and training by recording the detail of employee time spent. Project staff need to know how much employee time has been spent on assignments. Training staff need to know whether employees have actually attended course places booked for them.

Employees submit weekly time sheets to the time recording section. Time sheets include time spent on project tasks, time spent on training, unassigned time (holidays, meetings, sick leave) and dead time (time that was available for project work but not used).

2 3-schema Specification Architecture

2.1 The SSADM Rationale

ISE Library Volume Customising SSADM provides guidance for changes or extensions to SSADM. Any individual element of SSADM could be changed, extended or replaced. Nothing is sacrosanct. However, there is an underlying essence - what is really going on behind the techniques, products and names of steps in the Structural Model - that is summarised in the 3-schema Specification Architecture for specification and design as shown in Figure 2.1.

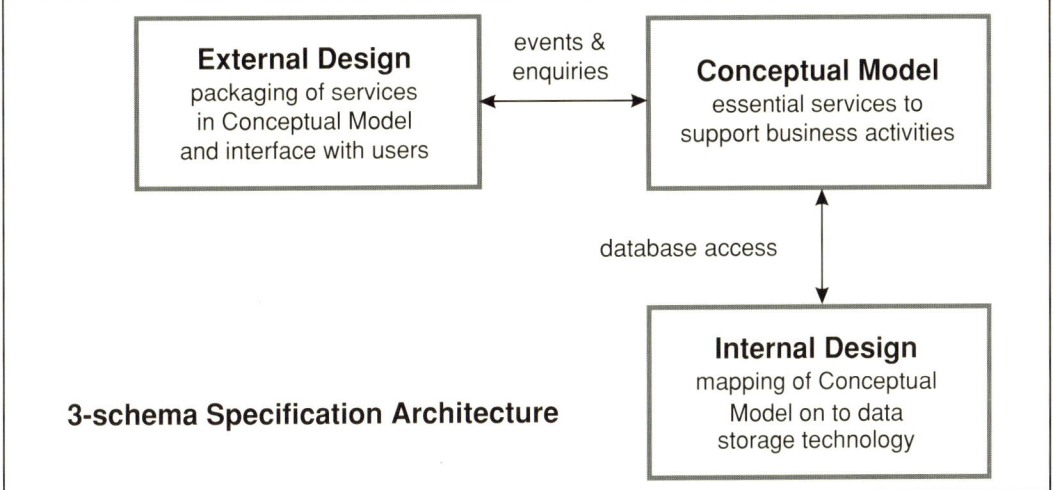

Figure 2.1: The three schemata of the 3-schema Specification Architecture

This 3-schema Specification Architecture does not address all of SSADM. It is concerned mainly with products of specification and design, and how they can be taken into implementation. And it provides a useful framework for application partitioning and integration.

First we need to understand more fully what it is and what it does.

2.2 The IT system is a simulation of the business

In the kinds of systems developed with SSADM, users require a database to act as a simulation of what is happening in their business. They can then use information obtained from the database to support decisions that are applied to the real world of the

21

business. It is easier and more effective to obtain information from the simulation than to deal directly with the real world.

Operating in the real world

In Projects-R-Us, for example, employees carry out assignments on projects. A project manager could go to a project site, identify tasks that need doing and tell employees to get the necessary materials and do the tasks. In practice, this approach works only for organisations with few concurrent projects, all managed by the same person - for example, a jobbing builder who does small projects like house extensions and kitchen refurbishments.

Operating via a database

For larger organisations it is more effective to:

- identify what needs doing by looking in the project file

- identify who is available by looking in the employee file

- define assignments by connecting employee and task records in the database. See Figure 2.2.

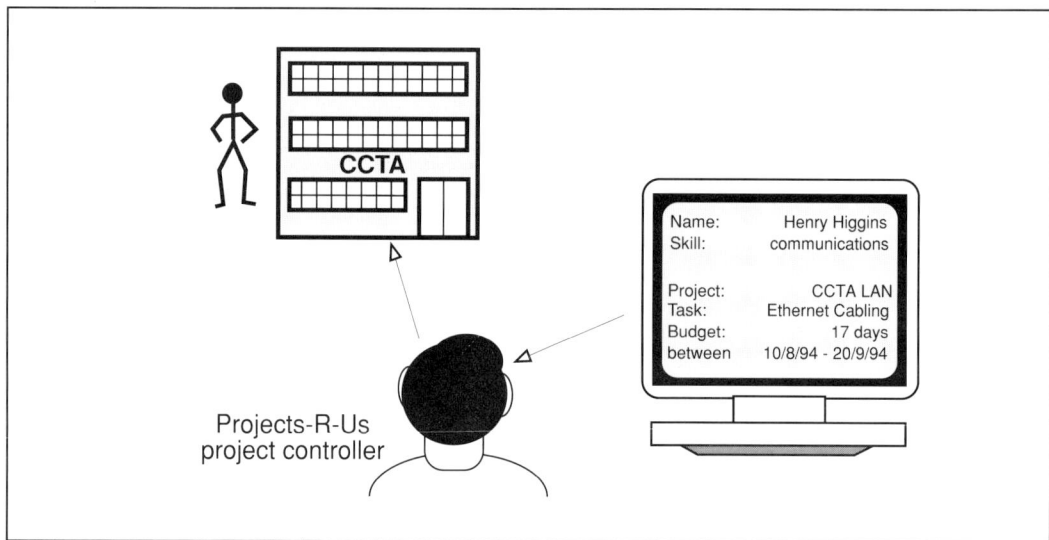

Figure 2.2: User bases real-world decisions on views of simulated reality

The decisions made in the database then lead to real-world action - real employees spend billable time and consume real materials in carrying out the assignments.

Scope of the IT system

Users do not want the entirety of their business to be simulated. Many aspects of the real world are not relevant to the business activities that need information support. We determine the scope of an IT system in two parts: defining information support needed for business activities, and deciding which business activities are to be automated. The results are the project's functional requirements, documented in the SSADM V4 Requirements Catalogue.

Business activities

Information support is needed for real-world business activities. In Projects-R-Us they would include: negotiating with clients, carrying out project tasks, deciding what resources are needed for tasks, recruiting employees.

How we document business activities is outside the scope of SSADM V4, but identifying what information support they need is the major part of SSADM Requirements Analysis.

Automated activities

We also need to decide whether any business activities can be wholly or partially automated. For example, in Projects-R-Us, the automated system might assign employees to tasks when employees with the required skills are available. The project manager would then have to deal only with exceptions - overriding some automatic assignments, negotiating with other project managers when no employees with required skills are available.

2.3 A Conceptual Schema for information support

The scope of an IT system is defined by the information support needed for the business. See Figure 2.3.

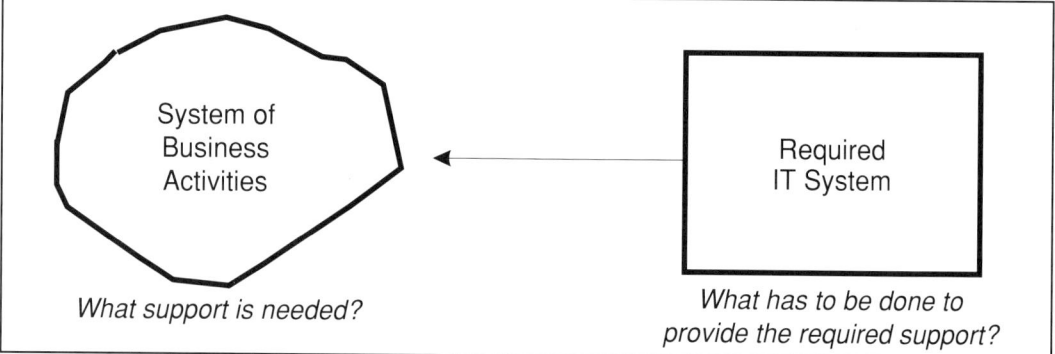

Figure 2.3: *Information support required by business determines scope of IT system*

In SSADM we specify provision of information support by:

- developing a Required System Logical Data Model from the entities and relationships within the scope of the business activities. Eventually, the LDM is turned into a database that simulates the behaviour of those entities and relationships.

- testing the LDM for its capability of providing information support - in SSADM terms, validating the data model - and producing enquiry access paths (EAPs) that document how the required outputs can be extracted from the LDM.

Content of the LDM

We can build up the attributes of the LDM entities as a result of this validation, informally (by asking for each entity as we develop an EAP, 'What attributes would be needed to support this output?') or formally, using Relational Data Analysis on the output specifications - usually both, in practice.

Updating the LDM

For the LDM to provide useful information support, it must be kept up-to-date. See Figure 2.4. We need to identify the changes in the business that have to be simulated in the LDM.

If we know what has to be in the LDM (to provide the outputs needed to support the business activities), we can find out what inputs are needed to keep it up-to-date.

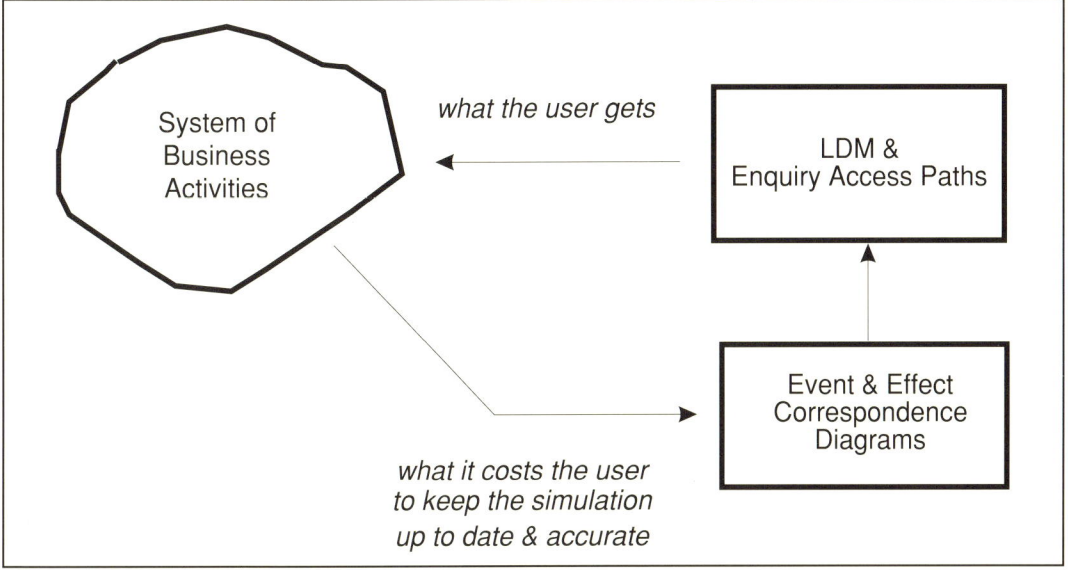

Figure 2.4: The simulation's usefulness to the business is dependent on it being kept up-to-date

Identifying events

We can analyse the LDM entities, attributes and relationships to identify what types of change/input are needed to keep the LDM up-to-date. There should be inputs for:

- the birth and death of every entity type; eg appointment and resignation of employee, definition and sign-off of task

- swapping of changeable relationships; eg an employee may move from one department to another; in contrast, a task cannot move from one project to another

- making and breaking of optional relationships; eg an employee's joining or leaving a training scheme

- changing every changeable attribute; eg a task's budget may be changed; in contrast, an employee's date of birth may not be changed (we exclude data entry errors from this level of modelling)

- imposing and removing constraints by setting states of entities; for example, an employee cannot join a training scheme while he is a member of another training scheme.

Each input is caused by an event in the business, eg appointment of employee, completion of task. We have to assign an event name to each type of change needed to update the LDM. In some cases event and LDM change will correspond one-to-one. However, some events will cause several changes, eg task rescheduling (before task start) can change task start date and task end date. Some changes may be caused by more than one event. For example, employee death, resignation and sacking may all be handled in the same way by the Projects-R-Us system.

Relating model to business	We must ensure that input is available for every type of event identified, and find out where in the business it comes from.

The important thing about this process is that it is one of discovery - we need to find out what information is needed to support business activities, how it could be provided from the LDM, what is needed to keep the LDM up-to-date, where we can obtain the inputs.

This part of the system description - LDM, EAPs and ECDs and their related products - we call the **Conceptual Schema**. It defines the services that have to be provided by the IT system, regardless of:

- what DBMSs the data will be stored in

- what kinds of workstations or styles of dialogue may be provided to users

- what combinations of services any given user may be permitted to use.

2.4 A 3-schema Specification Architecture

The **Conceptual Schema** defines the scope of the IT system, and its inputs from and outputs to the business. We also have to be concerned with an **External Schema**, that determines how users can access the system, and an **Internal Schema**, that maps the LDM on to a data storage technology and provides access to the stored data. See Figure 2.5. (Figure 2.5 uses the SSADM V4 abbreviations for Data Flow Diagrams - DFDs, Enquiry Process Models - EPMs, Update Process Models - UPMs and Process Data Interface - PDI.)

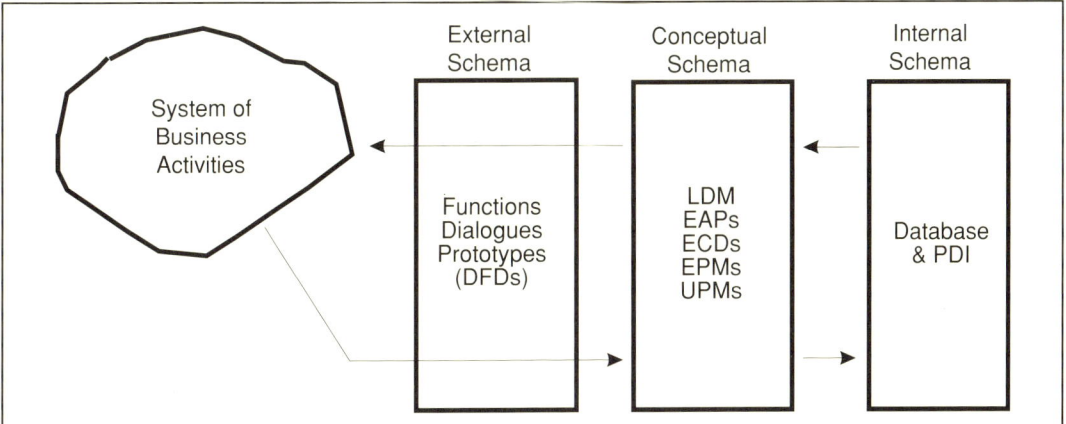

Figure 2.5: A 3-schema Specification Architecture

External Schema

In SSADM V4, the External Schema is defined in:

- functions (from DFDs and ad-hoc enquiry specifications)

- dialogues (perhaps developed via prototypes)

- the batch input-output subsystem.

The External Schema passes event data and enquiry triggers to the Conceptual Schema, and receives event and enquiry output in response. It has three major elements:

- a grouping of the events and enquiries in the Conceptual Schema into functions that serve user roles, plus the input structures that contain event data and enquiry triggers, and the output structures that contain event and enquiry response data

- for each function, processing to:

  - convert input structures to event and enquiry data

  - invoke event and enquiry processes

  - convert event and enquiry responses to output structures

  - detect and diagnose syntactic errors

  - report semantic errors notified by event processes

  - maintain and manipulate transient data

  - navigate between the elements of the function

  - transfer control to other functions

- a mapping of the External Schema logical specification to an implementation technology.

Discovery versus design	The External Schema differs from the Conceptual Schema in two significant ways. First, it is developed by design and engineering, not by discovery; second, there could be several different External Designs for a single Conceptual Schema.
	For the Conceptual Schema there is, within fairly narrow boundaries, a 'right' answer based on a data model that simulates the entities and relationships in the business to some required level of precision and currency. It is kept up-to-date by simulating business behaviour, by modelling events and updating the data model. We can properly call it a **Conceptual Model**, that has to be discovered by analysis.
Designed External Schema	There is no 'right' answer to be discovered for an External Schema. There are many factors outside the designer's control - allocation of user responsibilities within the business, level of ability and training of users, constraints on technology to be used, interface style guides, arbitrary rules and preferences, legislation.

The designer has to make trade-offs between conflicting requirements and constraints and construct a workable **External Design** acceptable to all users.

Multiple External Designs	There could be several External Designs for the same Conceptual Model. This is obviously true at the technology level. More-or-less the same external services could be delivered via, for example, Motif, MS-Windows, text menus, SQL-supported forms or batch input-output. In a distributed system these could all exist concurrently.
	But the differences could be more fundamental. The information support provided by a Conceptual Model could be packaged in different ways into functions, to serve different organisational structures and user roles. This is explored further in the *ISE Library Volume: Managing Reuse*.
IR dynamic user roles	The Inland Revenue has built support for this kind of multiple mapping into its system architecture. User role definitions are not embedded in the system specification. Instead, office managers can define roles locally for their own staff, and configure services provided by the Conceptual Model into packages that support them.
Internal Design	The Internal Schema is also developed by design rather than discovery; there could be more than one **Internal Design** for the same Conceptual Model. There are many DBMS technologies available to implement a Conceptual Model, and many ways to use their facilities to meet the physical system objectives in SSADM physical design. In a distributed system the same data model (or submodel) could be implemented (with replicated or partitioned instance data) at different locations, using different DBMSs.

2.5 **3-schema Specification Architecture and the SSADM Universal Function Model**

The 3-schema Specification Architecture is concerned with specification and design of the required system, especially the transition from logical design to physical design.

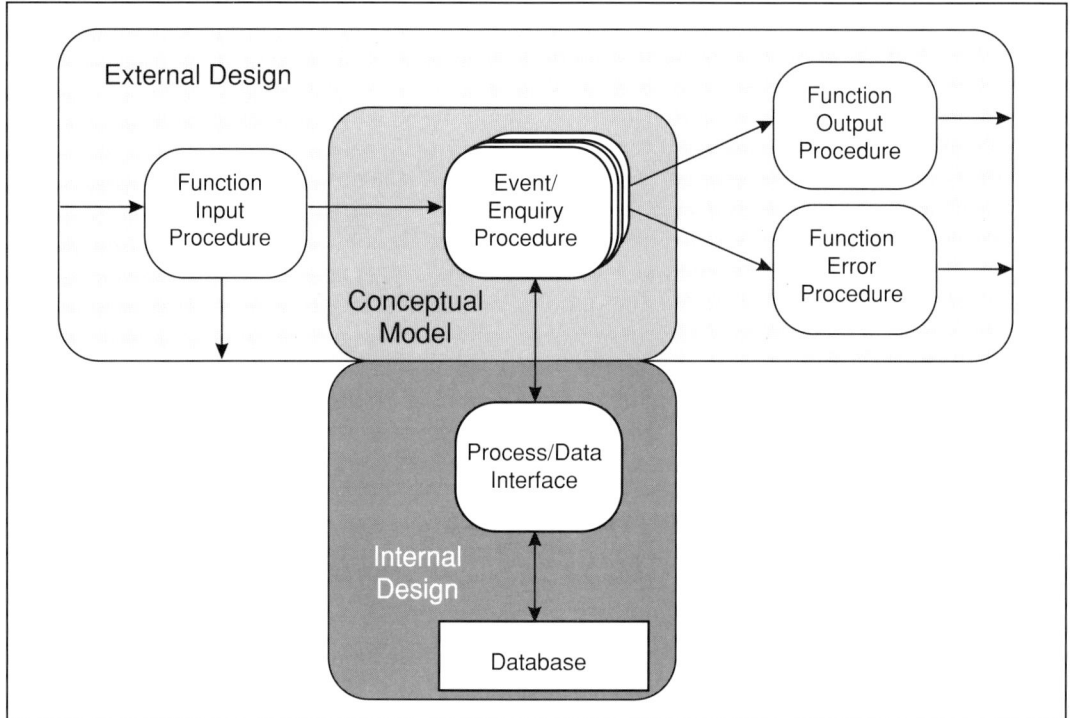

Figure 2.6: Mapping of SSADM universal function model to 3-schema Specification Architecture

The processing components of the 3-schema Specification Architecture are reflected in the SSADM universal function model. See Figure 2.6. Processes in each schema are implemented as code.

3 Aspects

3.1 'Aspect' as a view of an entity

LDM & real-world entities

An 'entity' on a logical data model is not an entity in the real world of the business. It is a logical data group that models a type of entity, and it models only those characteristics of the entity type that are of interest to the information system being described.

For example, 'Employee' on the LDM for Projects-R-Us models the real-world employee characteristics of identifier, name, department, seniority and training scheme. It does not model height, academic qualifications, home address or any other attributes and relationships of employees that are not of interest to the business area of Projects-R-Us for which IT support is being developed.

Pedantically, we could say that the LDM 'entity' defines an aspect (or view) of the real-world entity type, but usually there is no need. Most types of entity are in one-to-one correspondence with their LDM representations. We use the term 'entity' in the context of logical data modelling as shorthand for 'the logical data group that models the relevant view of a real-world entity type'.

Multiple perspectives

Some real-world entity types have to be modelled from more than one perspective. For example, in Projects-R-Us, employees are modelled from the perspective of working on projects and progressing through training schemes.

These two aspects of employee could be merged in the LDM of a single application that serves both perspectives. But if we want to develop separate applications, we need to model employee distinctly in each one (this does not imply that we have to implement separate databases).

Separate applications do not have to be integrated. We could, for example, develop separate systems for project control and training, and coordinate them through the real employee. ('Here are some possible training dates - how do they fit in with your project commitments?'). But if the applications are to be integrated we need to fit both aspects of employee into the integrated design.

Coordination of behaviour	When applications are integrated, aspects in different applications usually need to be coordinated; there are two possibilities. First, often there are shared characteristics. For example, project control and training management applications both need employee name and department, to be able to send outputs to the employee. Secondly, what has happened in one application may constrain what can be done in another. For example, when defining an employee's assignments, the project control application will need to ask the training management application for the dates of courses scheduled for the employee.
LDM representation	SSADM's logical data modelling accommodates aspects easily; they are LDM 'entities' with one-to-one relationships and can be represented as such.
Aspect birth & death	For development of ELHs and UPMs, it is simpler to assume that aspects are related in mandatory, one-to-one correspondence. It is possible to model aspects as having optional relationships, and define conditions under which they may gain and lose each other, but this usually adds complexity with no significant gains in design. We may compensate for this assumption in physical design, so that we do not create database records unnecessarily. See Chapter 7.
Related guidance	Aspects are used in other SSADM guides. The approach described in this volume is used in *ISE Library Volume: Distributed Systems: Application Development* to partition logical data models for different types of data processing location. In *ISE Library Volume: Reuse in SSADM using OO*, each aspect defines a separate object class - ie the

behaviour of one real-world entity type may be modelled over several related object classes.

3.2 Corporate entities and project aspects

Suppose, for example, that Projects-R-Us is one of three businesses - projects, management consultancy and software packages. They are run separately and have their own business and IT systems, but share their client base; many of the project clients also buy consultancy and packages.

The company that owns Projects-R-Us may decide to manage client data at corporate level. It makes sense for all three business areas to have consistent client information on current address, telephone number, credit rating etc. It may be useful to know in each system when there are problems with a client in other systems. And it may be possible to run marketing campaigns in one system, based on what we know about clients from other systems.

The entity defined in the Projects-R-Us Projects LDM is an **aspect** of the corporate client. It models client behaviour in the projects business. See Figure 3.1.

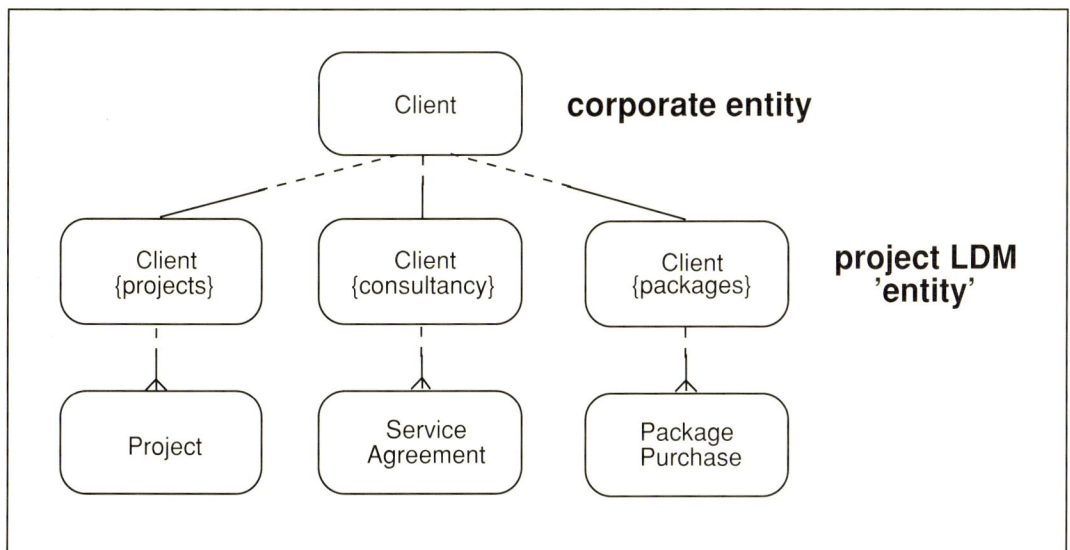

Figure 3.1: The three aspects of client

The effect of corporate aspects on the design of application databases depends on the implementation approach (decided as part of an IS strategy, not within a project). There are, broadly, two approaches:

- to copy down the corporate attributes into the application database. This leads to some replication of client information across applications but leaves each application self-contained, with one exception. When 'corporate' attributes are updated, a message must be fired off to the other systems, and similar messages may be received from other systems

- to have a corporate server for client information, serving all three systems. We have to take communication with the server into account when calculating costs, estimating performance and analysing robustness.

3.3 Project partitioning

Within a project, we may want to divide the LDM to support more-or-less self-contained subsystems. There might be three reasons for doing this:

- to allow detailed analysis and specification to proceed in parallel (this is an extension of the 'corporate entity' concept)

- to divide the project into subsystems to be delivered at different times (even if it is to be installed all in one place)

- to map the database (and invocations of event and enquiry processing) of the project on to different location types; subsystems for different types of location could, of course, be delivered at different times.

Where an entity type is needed in more than one subsystem we separate it into aspects.

For example, in Projects-R-Us we could (ignoring employee's department for a moment) partition employee allocation and scheduling into two

Chapter 3
Aspects

applications - project control and training - and define an aspect of employee in each as shown in Figure 3.2.

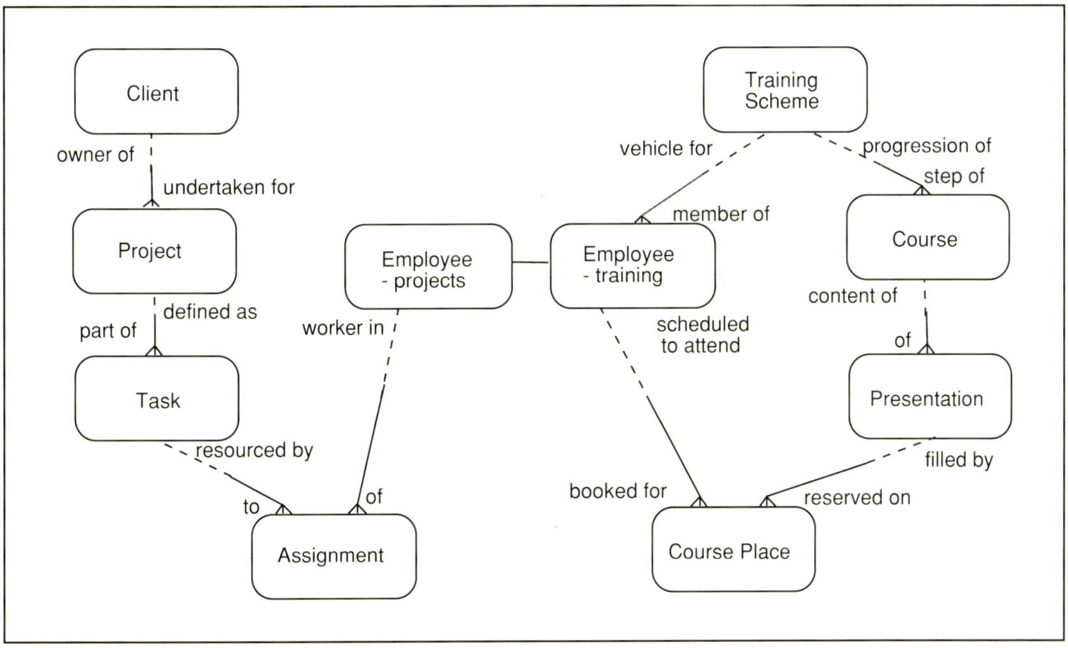

Figure 3.2: Project control and training aspects of employee

Separation of Employee into project control and training aspects simply separates the specification of employee behaviour (attributes, relationships and events) into two parts that can be modelled more-or-less independently of each other. It does not commit us to a physical mapping. For example:

- project control and training applications might be implemented on the same platform; Employee-projects and Employee-training might be implemented as separate physical files, or merged

- project control and training applications might be implemented in different places, each with its own Employee file.

Normalised aspects

We should examine whether the employee aspects overlap. For example, employee name and department will be needed in both project control and training

35

applications. We could normalise the shared attributes and relationships into a third aspect, which is effectively the basic existence of employee in Projects-R-Us, as shown in Figure 3.3.

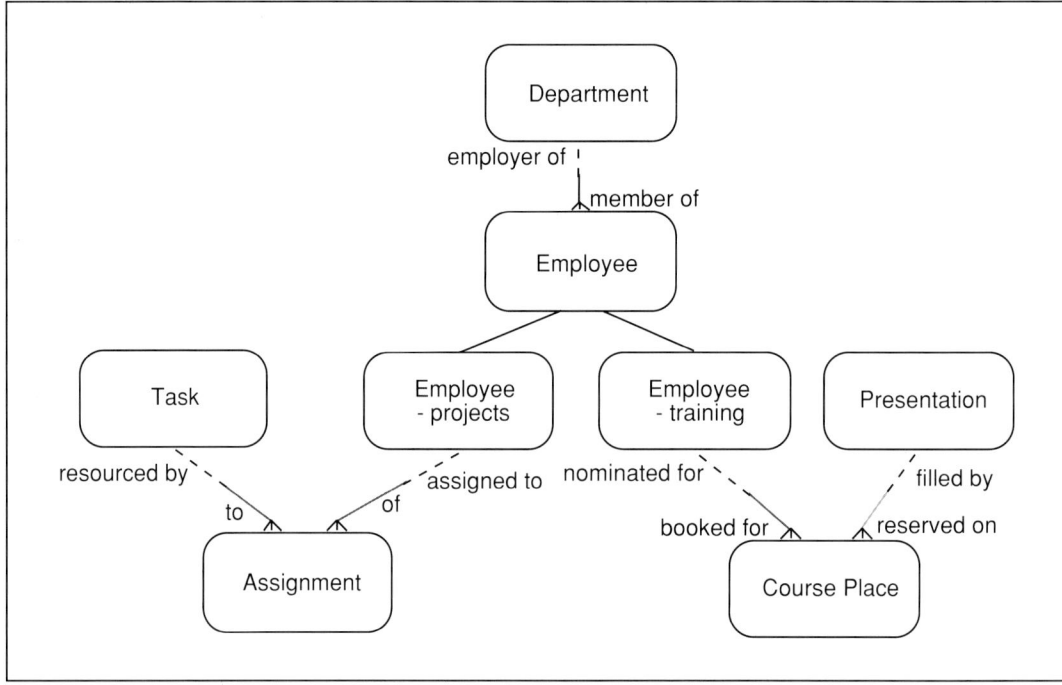

Figure 3.3: Shared aspects and relationships of employee separated out into base aspect

This is similar to the corporate aspect structure discussed in Section 3.2. It is a useful technique for analysis and logical design, and may be carried into implementation.

For example, suppose that the project control and training applications are to be implemented at different sites. Depending on requirements for performance, cost and robustness (the ability of the system to function when some locations are out of communication with the rest of the network) there would be different options for implementation:

- implement Employee (the basic aspect) and Department on a separate server that supports both applications. It could be located at the project control site, the training site, or some third location

- merge Employee and Department into one application; the other application would then make remote data requests

- replicate Employee and Department in both applications.

These, and other, options are discussed further in Chapter 7, Internal Design.

3.4 Different behaviours (parallel lives)

When a project LDM has been divided into subsystem LDMs, any entity (including a partitioned aspect) may have asynchronous cycles in its behaviour. In entity-event modelling terms, it has parallel lives.

For example, in Projects-R-Us there are two interleaved, asynchronous cycles within Task.

- task scheduled end date and budget may be changed at any time up to end of task; task scheduled start date may be changed at any time up to actual start of task

- task may have only one 'live' assignment at a time, but it may gain or lose its current assignment at any time.

Rather than develop a parallel life ELH for Task we could separate Task into two aspects as shown in Figure 3.4.

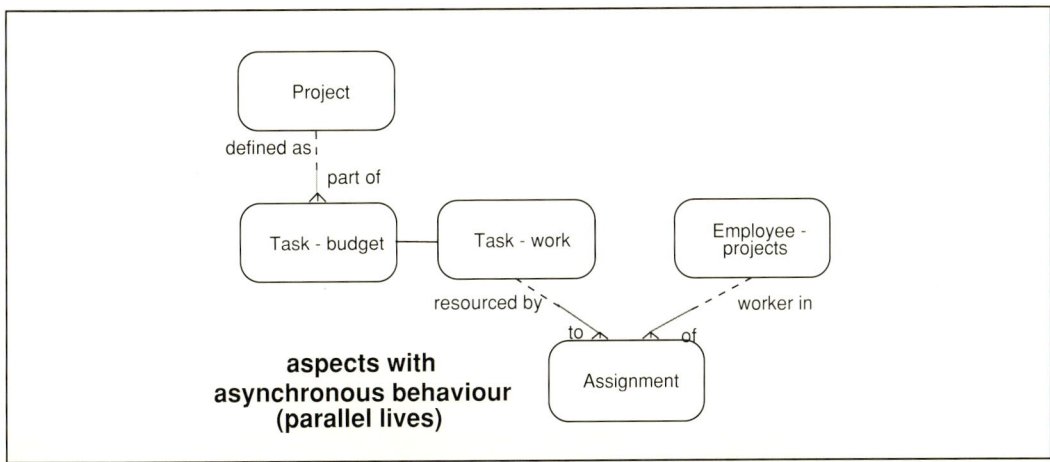

Figure 3.4: Asynchronous behaviour (parallel lives) of Task separated into aspects

This would allow the budget behaviour of Task to be located separately from (eg on a central resource management database, supporting resource demand smoothing across all projects) or delivered earlier or later than the assignments behaviour.

3.5 What is an aspect?

An aspect is an application's view of a real-world entity type, modelling part of its behaviour. What we usually call 'an entity' on an LDM is really an aspect, since it represents only a partial view of the real-world entity type. In most cases a real-world entity type has only one LDM aspect; there is no confusion in referring to 'LDM entities'. We need to distinguish aspects only when there are multiple views of the same entity that have to be coordinated in some way.

An entity type has a 'basic existence' aspect, represented by its primary key (and, if its key is hierarchical, the corresponding master relationship). Other aspects are constrained by the birth and death of the basic aspect. In theory, every other attribute and relationship could be modelled as a separate aspect. In practice, this is rarely useful. Our approach is to keep aspects as large as possible, and split them only when the real-world entity has distinct behaviours that need to be modelled separately - for example, when it has to be represented in different applications or has parallel lives within an application. Shared attributes can reside in the basic aspect.

In theory, an entity cannot have two aspects; it should have one, or three or more. If it has one behaviour that needs to be separated from its basic existence, it should have another behaviour that is distinct from its basic aspect. In Projects-R-Us, Task has parallel lives for budgeting and work. Both of these should be tied to Task's basic aspect, which models a task's existence as part of a project. See Figure 3.5.

In many cases in practice, basic existence can be merged with another aspect without causing any problems. In Projects-R-Us, Task and Task-budget are merged.

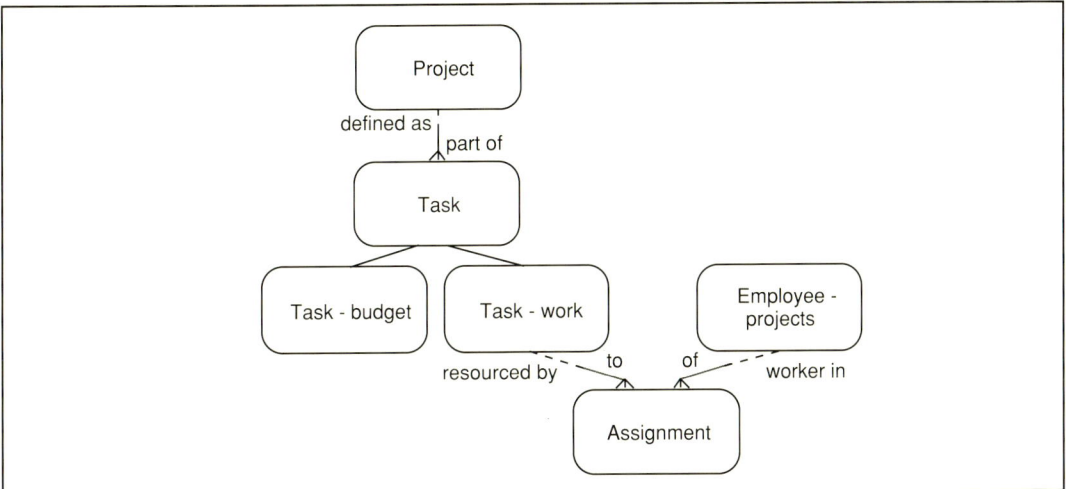

Figure 3.5: In theory Task cannot have just two aspects

3.6	Aspects and inheritance

Using aspects gives a consistent way of modelling entity behaviour from corporate model to entity within subsystem. For example, Figure 3.6 illustrates a possible hierarchy of Client aspects in Projects-R-Us.

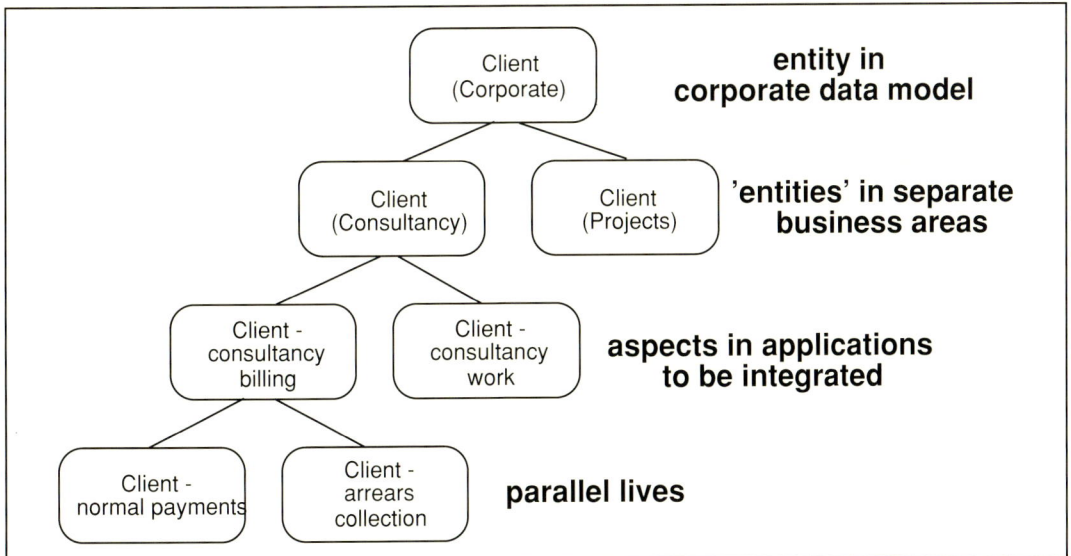

Figure 3.6: A possible hierarchy of client aspects in Projects-R-Us

Aspects and aggregation	It is easy to visualise how an aspect within a project could inherit the data and processes of its corporate entity, or how, say, the normal payments aspect of Client could inherit the data and processes of the consultancy billing aspect. However, pictures like the one in Figure 3.6 must not be confused with subtype hierarchies (class hierarchies in OO). One-to-one relationships 'coming down' a subtype hierarchy are mutually exclusive. All aspects of a single entity instance can exist concurrently. And (in theory, at least) an entity aspect can invoke any other aspect of the same entity in event or enquiry processing. This is a restricted version of the OO concept of aggregation - the restriction being that all the aspects are views of the same real-world entity. (Aggregation, as it is usually described in the OO literature, also accommodates the construction of aggregates of different types of entity.)
Aspects and subtypes	In a sense, defining entity aspects is the opposite of defining entity sub- and supertypes, and both are useful in partitioning a business area into applications. With sub- and super-types we identify similar behaviour of different real-world entity types. This behaviour should be modelled within one application. For example, project workers could be employees or contractors. Every instance of project worker would be either an employee or a contractor. We would want to model the 'project worker' behaviour of employees and contractors in the same application as shown in Figure 3.7. With aspects we identify different behaviours of the same real-world entity type. These behaviours can be modelled in different applications. For example, a contractor works on projects and has contracts with Projects-R-Us. There are interactions between the two behaviours that need to be coordinated: • the contractor name and address is needed in both behaviours • a contractor should not be working on projects unless they have a current contract.

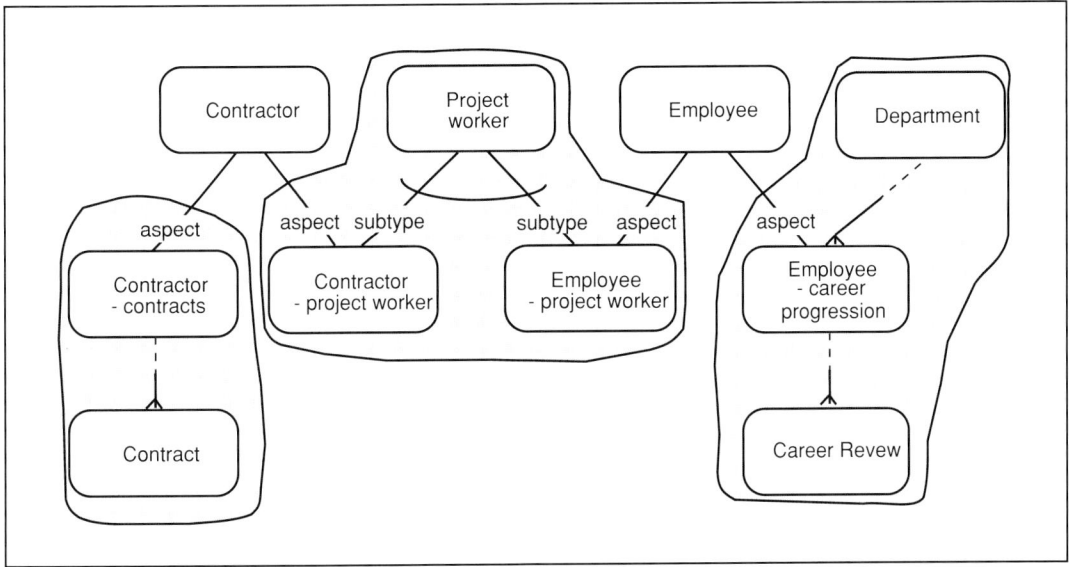

Figure 3.7: Potential for three applications based on similar behaviour of different real-world entities

Apart from these interactions the behaviours are largely independent. A contract could span several projects, a new contract could be made part-way through a project, contract terms could be changed at any time. Provided that the interactions are handled, we could model contractor in separate applications for project work and contracts. Similarly, we could model employee in separate applications for project work and career progression.

4 Partitioning the Conceptual Model

4.1 Summary of approach

We start with two inputs:

- a business area whose activities can be partitioned so that they can be supported by separate applications

- an overview LDM for the business area. This might have been developed as part of an IS strategy, it might be extracted from a corporate data model or we might have to develop it specifically.

The LDM has to be partitioned according to the scope of each application. Entities needed in more than one application are represented as separate aspects in the partial LDMs.

We shall develop a distinct Conceptual Model - attributes, process models, event and enquiry inputs and outputs - for each application. First, we develop ELHs and EAPs for each application, coordinating the applications in two ways:

- where an event spans more than one application, we use the same event name in both

- we identify where an enquiry is needed in one application to support an event or enquiry in another application; there may be opportunities to create reusable enquiry processes.

We may identify further aspects of LDM entities to be modelled in parallel ELHs.

The completion of the Conceptual Model for each application and the integration of the models are described in Chapter 5.

4.2 Identification of separately isolable areas of a data model

User driven

In some cases the applications are specified in advance; this would be the case if we were running multiple projects within a programme. Applications might be implied by the organisation structure. For example, Projects-R-Us has separate sections that control projects and manage training, with very limited interaction.

Where application boundaries are not so clear-cut, we need to identify possible applications and agree them with the users. This might be the case if we were partitioning a large project into subsystems to be developed in parallel.

Soft Systems approach

The Soft Systems Methodology (SSM) can be used with SSADM; [see *ISE Library Volume: Applying Soft Systems Methodology to an SSADM Feasibility Study*] in an SSADM Feasibility Study. SSM uses the concept of a human activity system that needs information support, which may be provided by an IT system.

A human activity system is a coherent set of activities and the logical dependencies between them; it describes what has to be done in a business, as distinct from who does it and how it is done.

Human activity systems are decomposed by the requirements of performance monitoring and control action. A subsystem is a subset of the activities for which, as a group, we can define measures of performance, monitor the activities and take control action where necessary.

We can use these ideas to identify areas of business activity that can be separately monitored and controlled. For example, suppose that Projects-R-Us were organised differently, so that project managers were responsible for ensuring that staff working for them also made progress through the training schemes. The application areas would not be implied by the organisation structure. The requirements for monitoring and control of project management activities and training management activities are different - this would suggest two distinct application areas.

Chapter 4
Partitioning the Conceptual Model

Types of location | Distinct applications may be needed to support local activities in different types of business location. This is a major factor if the IT system is to be distributed, [see *ISE Library Volume: Distributed Systems: Application Development*], but may also be a requirement of a centralised IT system.

Secondary applications | We might call the applications that support business activity the primary applications. Some applications do not directly support business activity, but provide support for those that do. Typically there are two types:

- shared servers, providing primary applications with common data on shared entities - as described in 'normalised aspects' in Chapter 3. In Projects-R-Us, both project control and training management need employee data (name, department etc)

- updating support, where the users are agents of the IT system; their business activity is keeping the Conceptual Model up-to-date for primary applications. In Projects-R-Us, the time recording section inputs data used by project control and training management, but has no primary business role.

Entity-event matrix | The overview LDM may be fairly well-developed, with many attributes defined. This could be the case if it were extracted from a corporate data model, or a if a decision were taken part-way through a project to split it into subsystems for detailed design and implementation.

Without developing full ELHs, it is possible to identify events for each entity and draw an entity-event matrix as shown in Figure 4.1. The questions to be asked for identification of events were given in Section 2.3.

If the matrix is of manageable size, and in a form that can be easily manipulated (eg exported to a spreadsheet), it may be possible to identify clusters of events and entities that indicate self-contained applications.

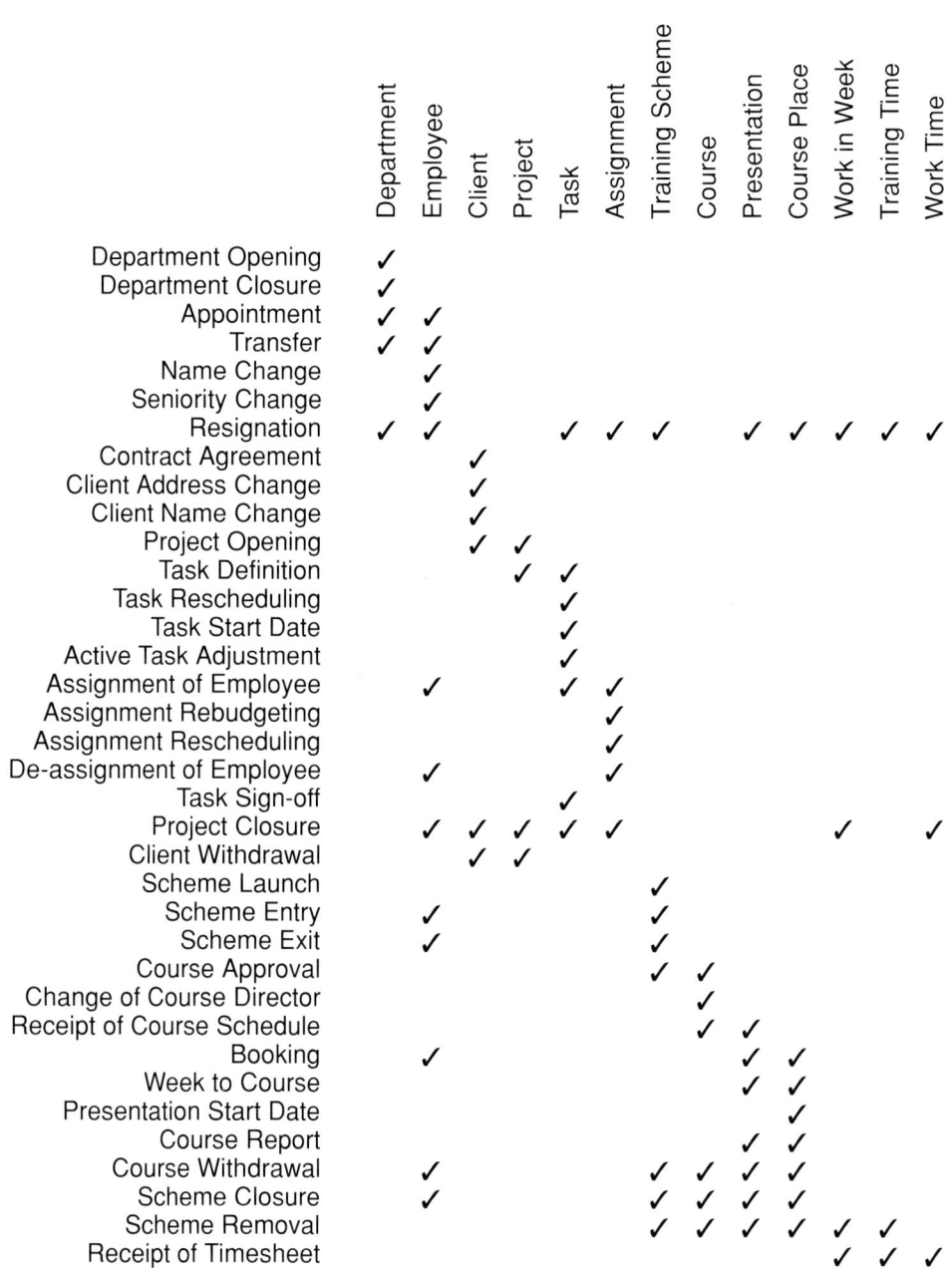

Figure 4.1: Projects-R-Us entity-event matrix

Chapter 4
Partitioning the Conceptual Model

This approach is also used in the *ISE Library Volume: Distributed Systems: Application Development* for partitioning the project LDM for distribution options (part of the Business System Options). A practical problem is the possible size of the matrix. One possibility is that facilities could be built into CASE tools to analyse entity-event cross-references to identify clusters.

Corporate data model

There is a widely-held view that application areas can easily be identified by inspection of a corporate data model. In practice this seems not to be true.

A corporate data model may provide a rich LDM for the overview of the whole business area, but it describes a static picture of entities, relationships and attributes. Applications also need to capture the behaviour of entities - the enquiries they have to serve and the events that update them.

Separation of different behaviours of real-world entities leads to self-contained applications with relatively simple integration. Usually, the different behaviours of an entity are not directly derivable from its data definitions in a corporate data model.

4.3 Using aspects to decompose and isolate areas of a data model

From the discussion in Section 4.2 it is apparent that we can partition the Projects-R-Us LDM into three application areas: project control, training and time recording, plus a shared server for employee data. We shall do this by splitting shared entity types into separate aspects. See Figure 4.2.

Benefit of approach

The benefit of doing this is that each application will have a complete data model. SSADM development can proceed largely independently for each. The only relationships to be managed between applications are one-to-one relationships between aspects of the same entity - the simplest relationships we can model in LDMs. We shall integrate processing in ECDs and EAPs on these one-to-one relationships.

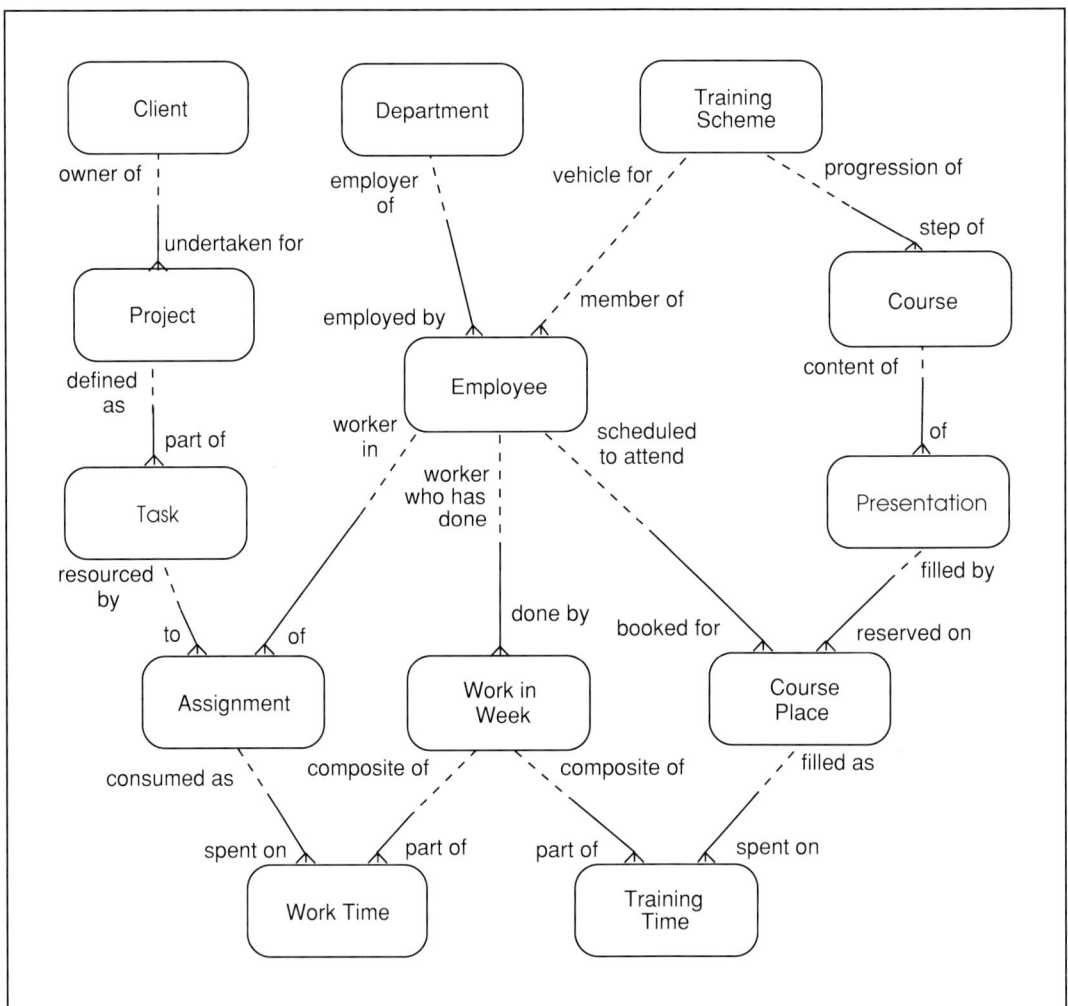

Figure 4.2: Projects-R-Us LDM

Defining aspects

There are three shared entity types:

- employee - needed in all three applications plus the shared server

- assignment - needed in projects and time recording

- course place - needed in training and time recording.

We could define the basic existence of each shared entity type, and then define a separate aspect for each relationship on the LDM as for Employee in Figure 4.3.

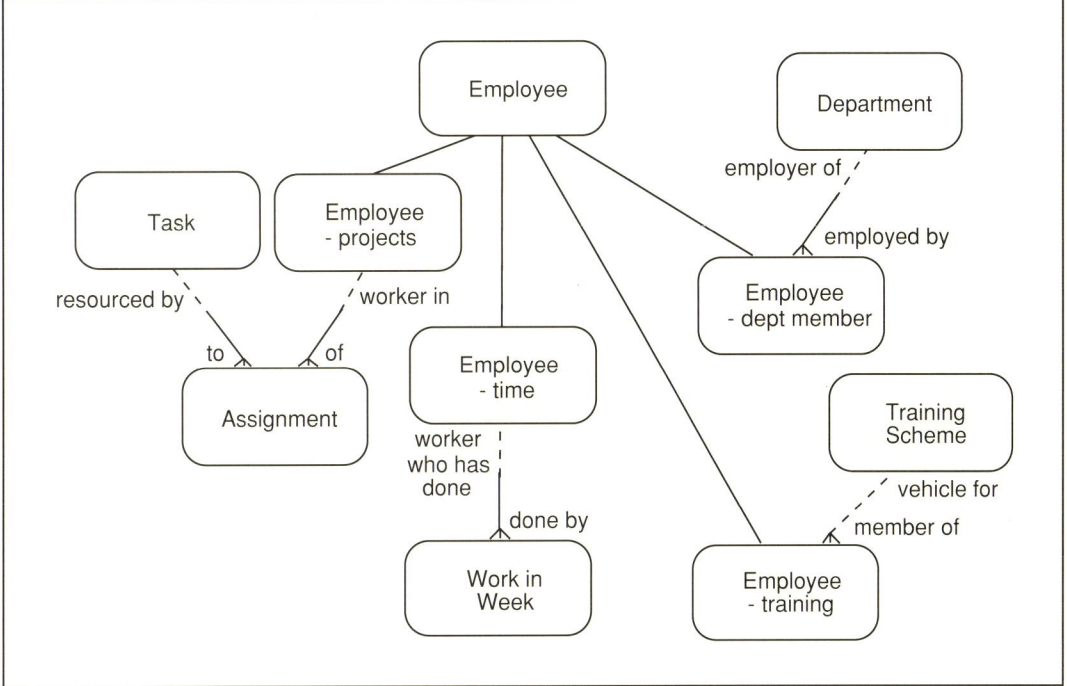

Figure 4.3: Employee basic existence and aspects defined for each relationship

We could go even further and define a separate aspect for each changeable non-derived attribute, such as employee address, but there would seem to be no benefit in doing so.

Figure 4.4 shows the LDM for Projects-R-Us partitioned into the three application areas discussed earlier plus a shared server for the employee data. The base aspects of Assignment and Course Place are placed respectively in the project control and training application areas.

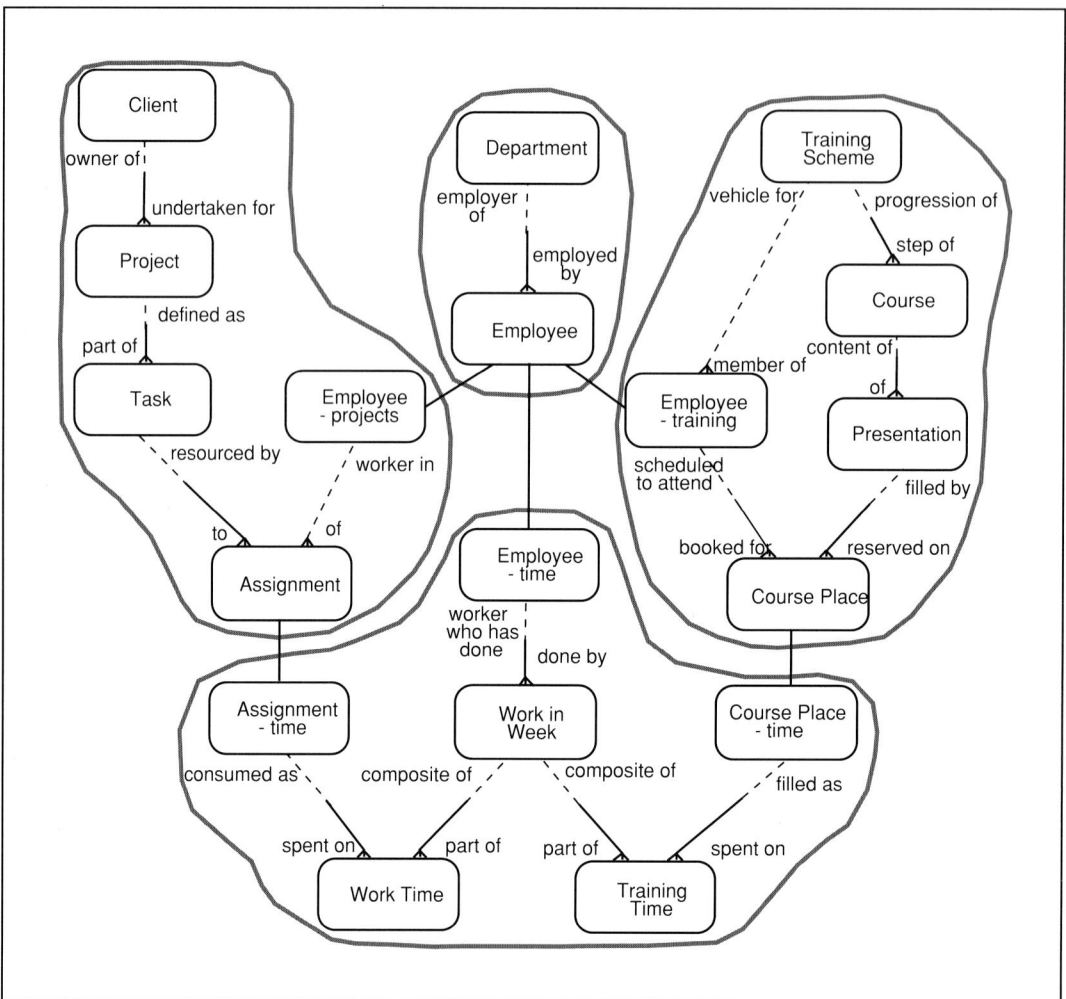

Figure 4.4: Partitioned LDM for Projects-R-Us

There is no requirement to retain previous departments for employees, so the Department-member aspect of Employee has not been separately modelled in the LDM in Figure 4.4.

Note: it is possible to optimise the implementation of a shared server by merging it with one of the primary applications, usually the first to be implemented. This is discussed further in Chapter 8, Issues.

Chapter 4
Partitioning the Conceptual Model

Duplication of relationships

The time recording application of the LDM contains Employee, Assignment and Course Place. There is a relationship between Employee and Assignment in the project control application, and one between Employee and Course Place in the training application. We need to decide whether these relationships should be duplicated in time recording, giving the LDM shown in Figure 4.5.

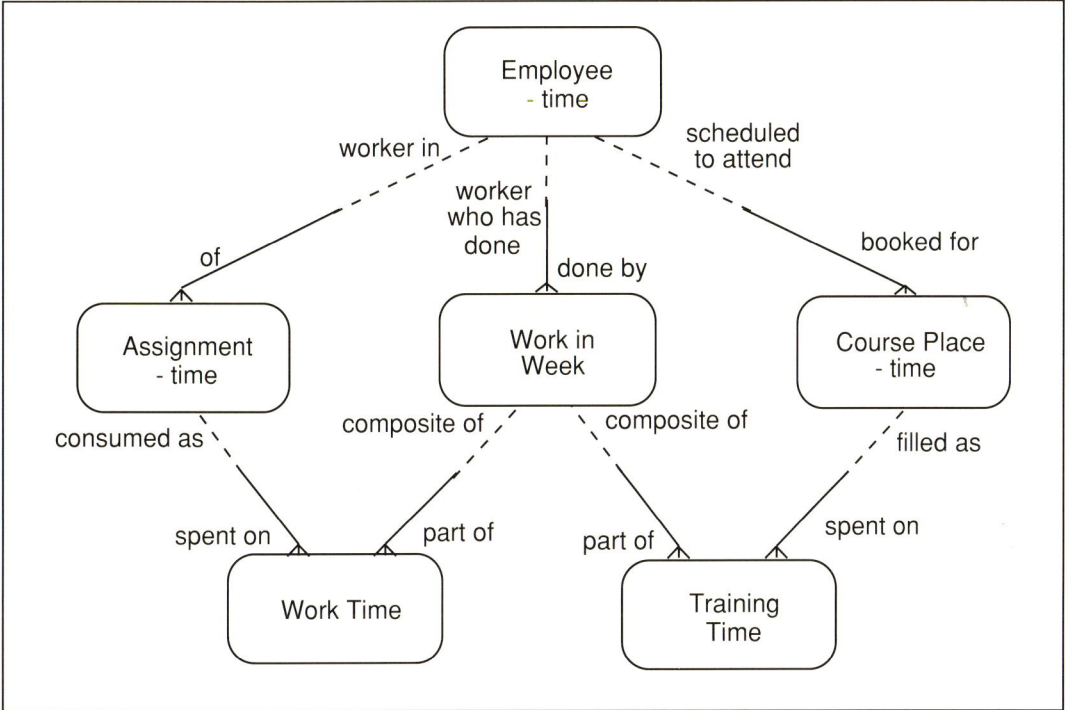

Figure 4.5: Time recording LDM with two relationships duplicating those in other applications

The first question to be asked is 'Can these relationships be changed by events that originate within the scope of this application?'. If they can, they need to be in this LDM.

If they cannot, then, ideally, they should not be in this LDM. However, we also have to ask 'Will the applications that manage these relationships be in place before this one?'. If not, we should include the relationships in this LDM, even though it will mean that, when all applications have been developed, the modelling of the relationships will have been duplicated.

In Projects-R-Us, Assignments are defined in the project application and their relationships with Employee-projects are fixed - an assignment is an association between an employee and a task; it cannot be switched to another employee. Similarly, the relationship between Employee-training and Course Place is managed within the training application. Time recording is to be implemented after projects and training. There is no need to duplicate the relationships.

4.4 Developing enquiry views

We need to validate the LDMs for each application, to ensure that they can deliver the outputs needed to support business activities. The procedure is similar to that for a single LDM except that we have to identify where enquiries cross application boundaries.

In Projects-R-Us, projects staff need to know:

- the availability of employees

- the status of tasks within a project (not started, in progress, completed), and whether employees are currently assigned

- how much time has been spent on tasks; for tasks in progress, time spent as a proportion of budget.

Some enquiries are contained within a single application. For example, Status of Tasks in a Project, as shown in Figure 4.6.

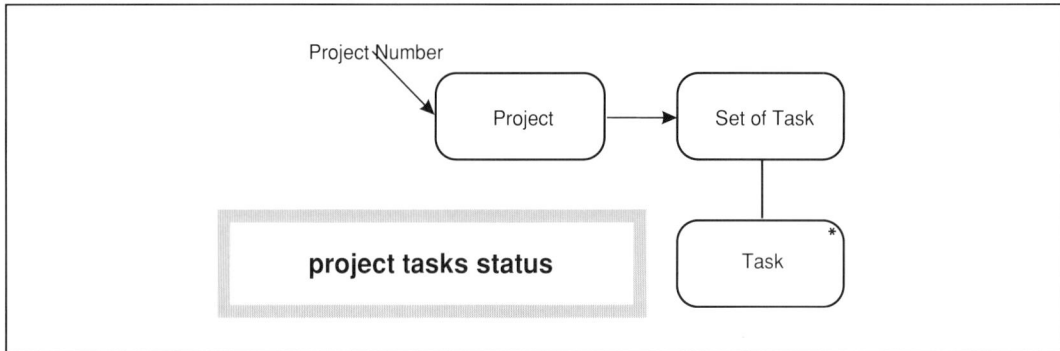

Figure 4.6: EAP for status of tasks in a project

Using shared attributes

Some enquiries are apparently within the scope of one application, but need shared attributes that are maintained in another application, often a shared server. For example, we have to be able to report which employees are working on a project. See Figure 4.7.

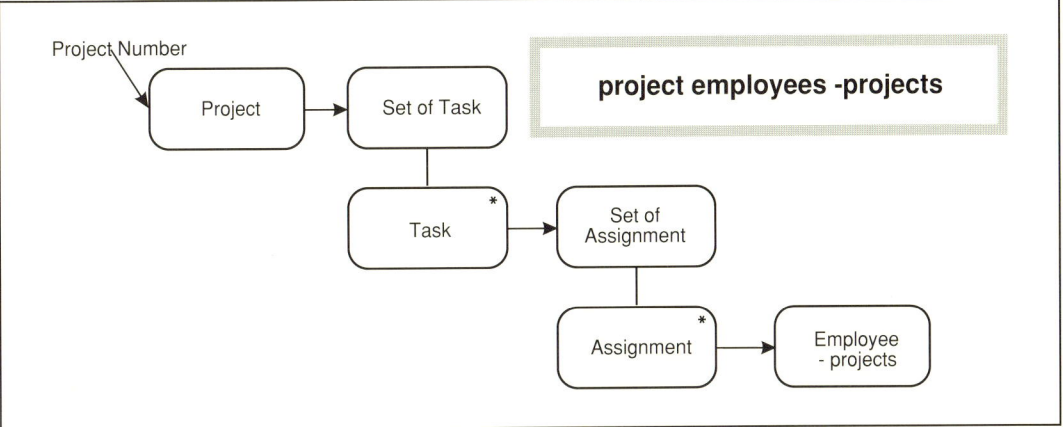

Figure 4.7: Employees working on a project - projects enquiry fragment

If we also need to report Employee Name, we have to obtain it from the shared server. See Figure 4.8.

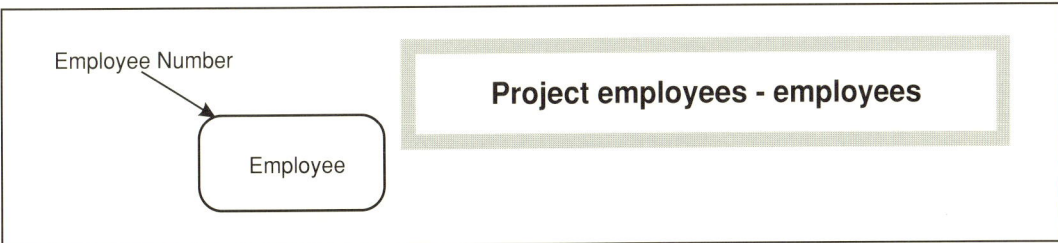

Figure 4.8: Employees working on a project - employees enquiry fragment

Similarly, the list of employees scheduled to attend a course presentation needs Employee Name. See Figures 4.9 and 4.10.

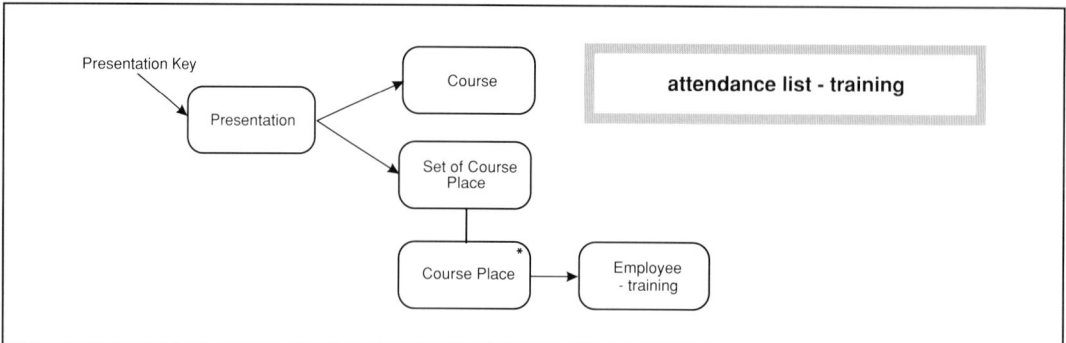

Figure 4.9: Scheduled attendance list for course presentation - training enquiry fragment

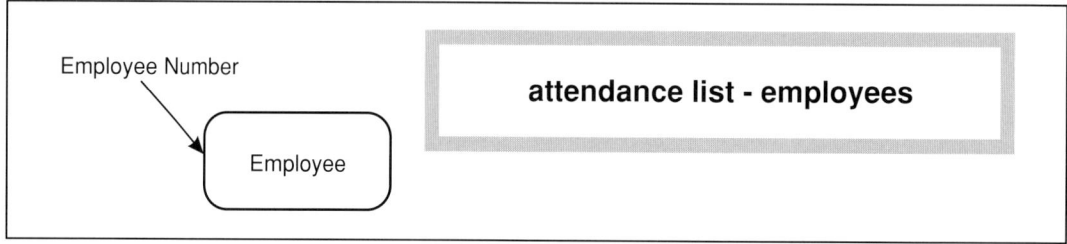

Figure 4.10: Scheduled attendance list for course presentation - employees enquiry fragment

Reusable enquiry fragments

Some enquiry fragments are reusable. For example, instead of defining a separate Employee Name fragment for each enquiry that needs an employee's name, we can define a single fragment to be invoked wherever Employee Name is needed, as shown in Figure 4.11.

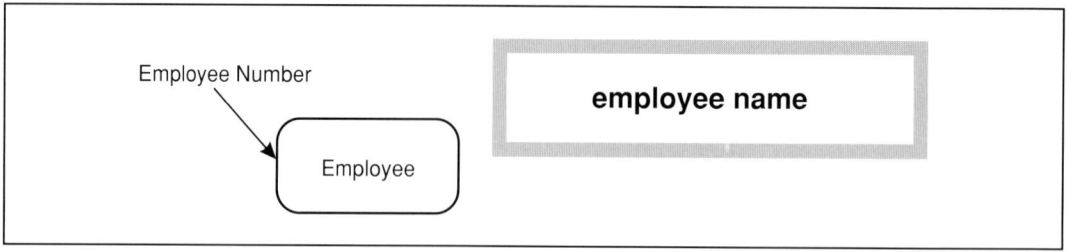

Figure 4.11: Reusable enquiry fragment - employee name

Enquiries that span applications

Some enquiries cross application boundaries. We need to develop a separate fragment for each application. For example, work done on a project spans the project control and time recording applications, as shown in Figures 4.12 and 4.13.

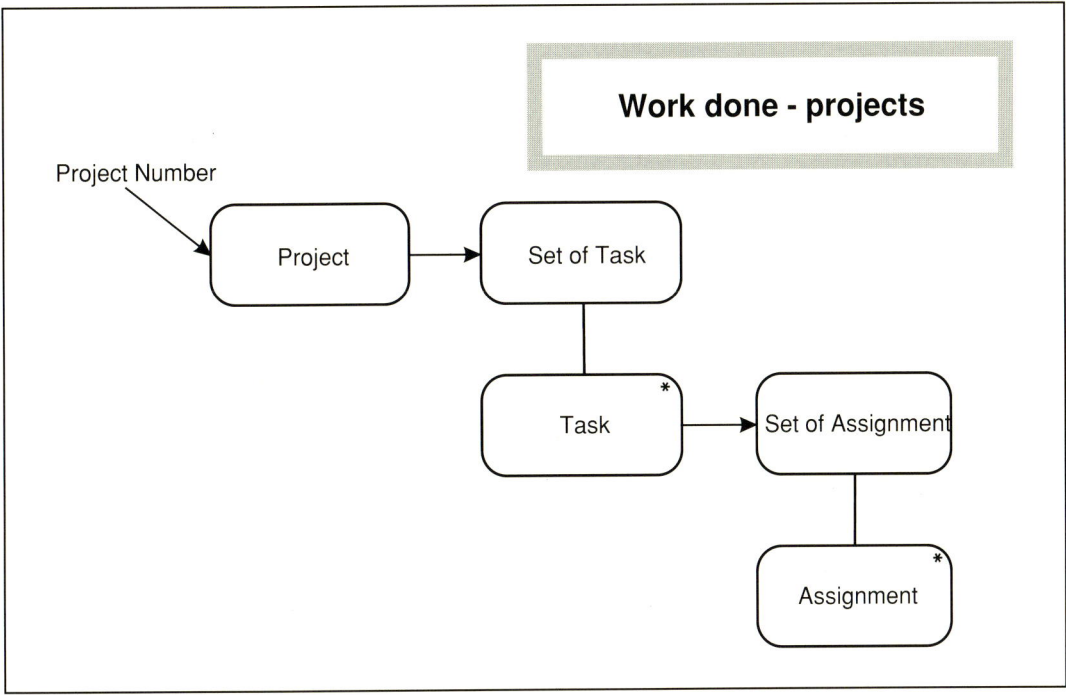

Figure 4.12: Work done on a project - projects enquiry fragment

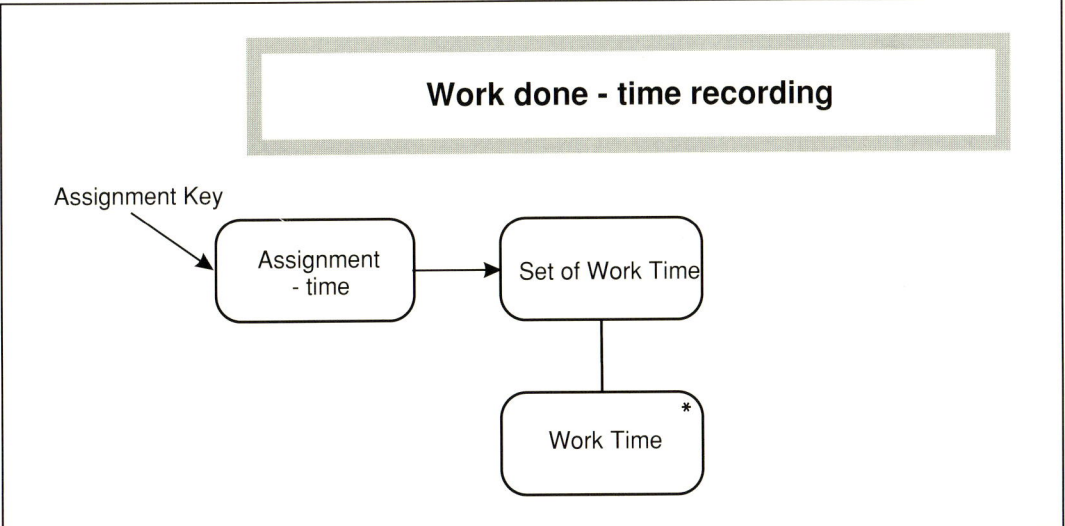

Figure 4.13: Work done on a project - time recording enquiry fragment

The separation of Employee into aspects means that, from the application view, each fragment of the enquiry is self-contained and complete. The connection between the fragments will be defined when we link EAPs or create EPMs.

Enquiries on shared entities

Common attributes for a shared entity can be modelled in a shared server, which is invoked to provide reference data for enquiries and updates that originate in one application. However, some enquiries are needed in more than one application. The entry point for such enquiries is the shared aspect. For example, an enquiry on employee commitments is needed in both project control and training management, but in order to pick up all commitments the entry point must be the shared aspect. See Figures 4.14 to 4.16.

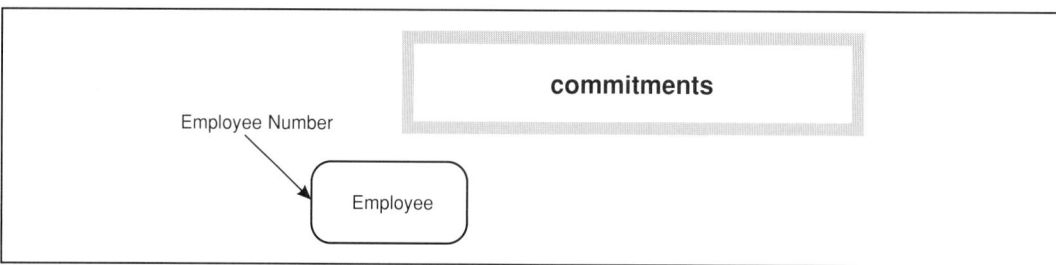

Figure 4.14: Employee commitments - entry point is shared aspect of employee

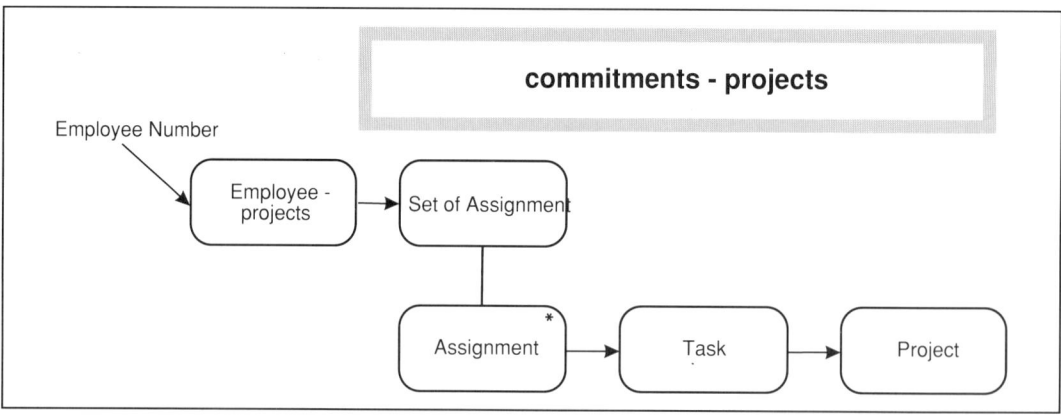

Figure 4.15: Employee commitments - projects

Chapter 4
Partitioning the Conceptual Model

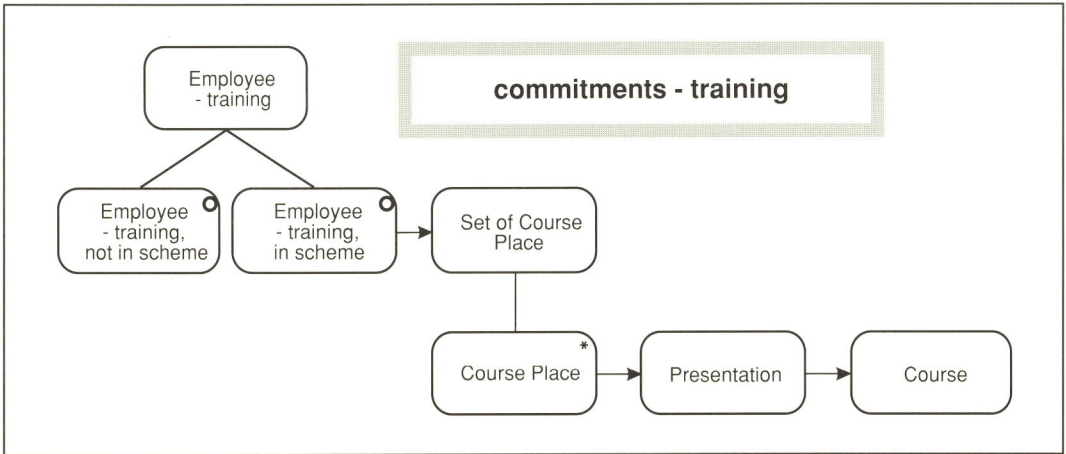

Figure 4.16: Employee commitments - training

Note that we do not have to develop an enquiry view across several applications as a single task. We need to define what each application will contribute to it, and deal with presentation of the combined results as part of the External Design.

Extending general enquiries

One advantage of basing a general enquiry on the shared aspect (rather than trying to invoke it from different places within primary applications) is that further aspects may be easily added to it. For example, Projects-R-Us might decide in the future to record other employee commitments (eg unavailable time due to holidays, medical treatment etc) in the time recording application. The LDM would be as shown in Figure 4.17.

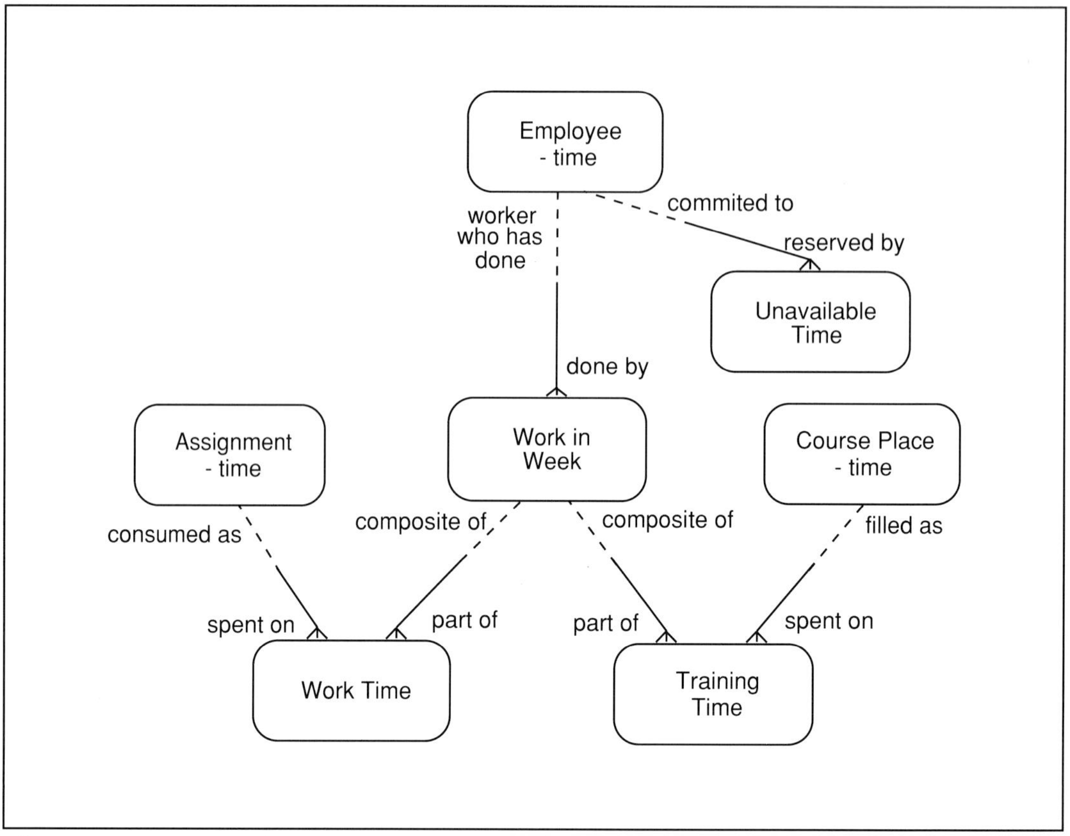

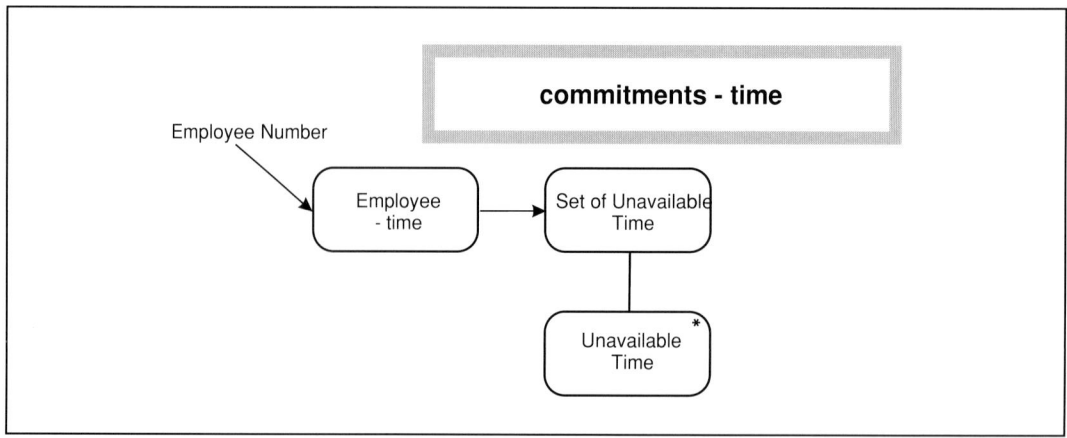

Figure 4.17: Time recording LDM with unavailable time added

It is then very easy to add a further component to the commitments enquiry, as shown in Figure 4.18.

Figure 4.18: Employee commitments - time

Chapter 4
Partitioning the Conceptual Model

4.5 Developing entity life histories

We can develop ELHs independently within each application, provided that events are named consistently across the applications. For example, see the respective shared server, project control, time recording and training ELHs for Employee aspects in Figures 4.19 to 4.22.

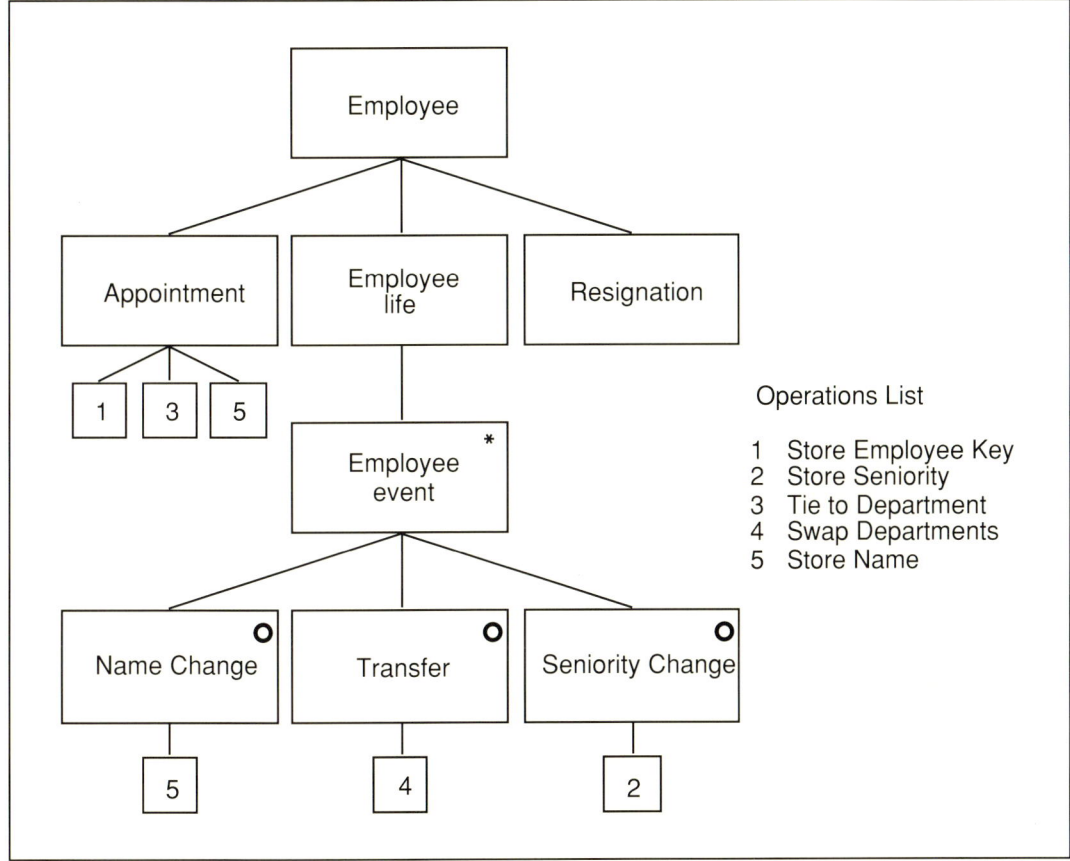

Figure 4.19: ELH for base aspect of employee

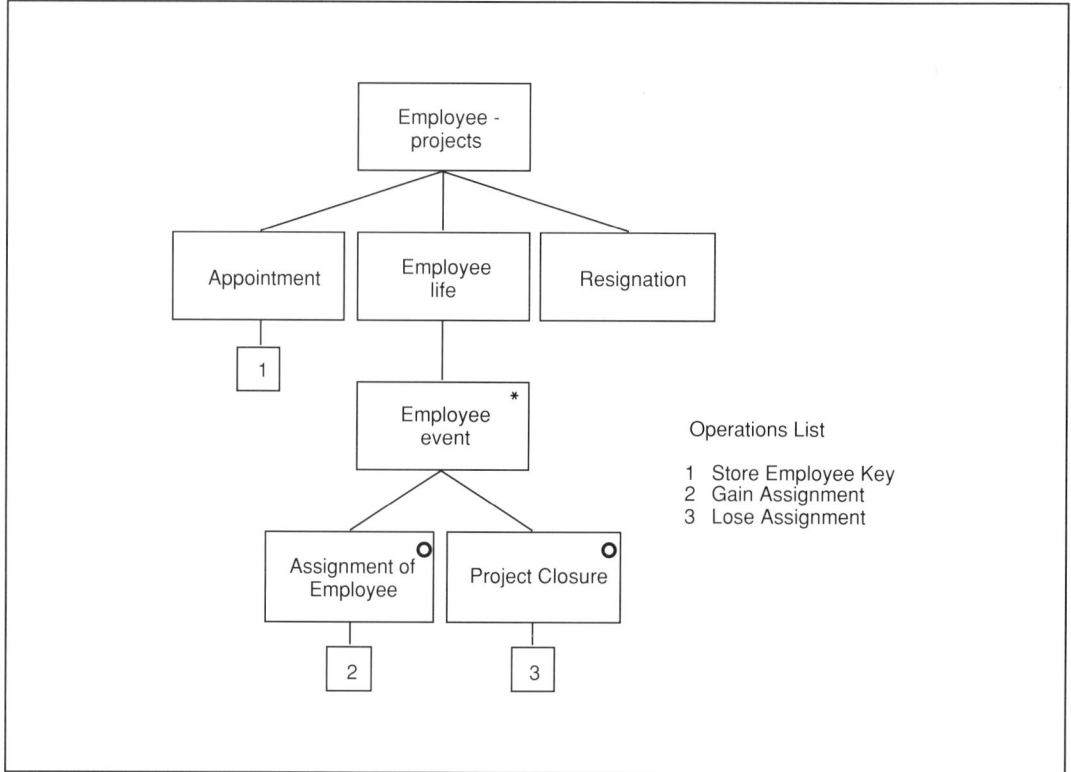

Figure 4.20: ELH for projects aspect of employee

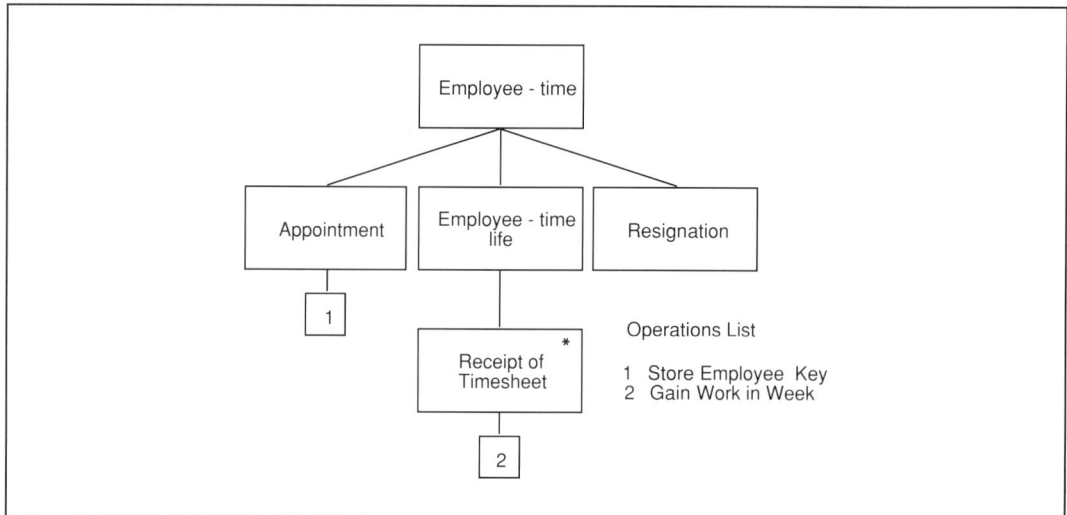

Figure 4.21: ELH for time recording aspect of employee

Chapter 4
Partitioning the Conceptual Model

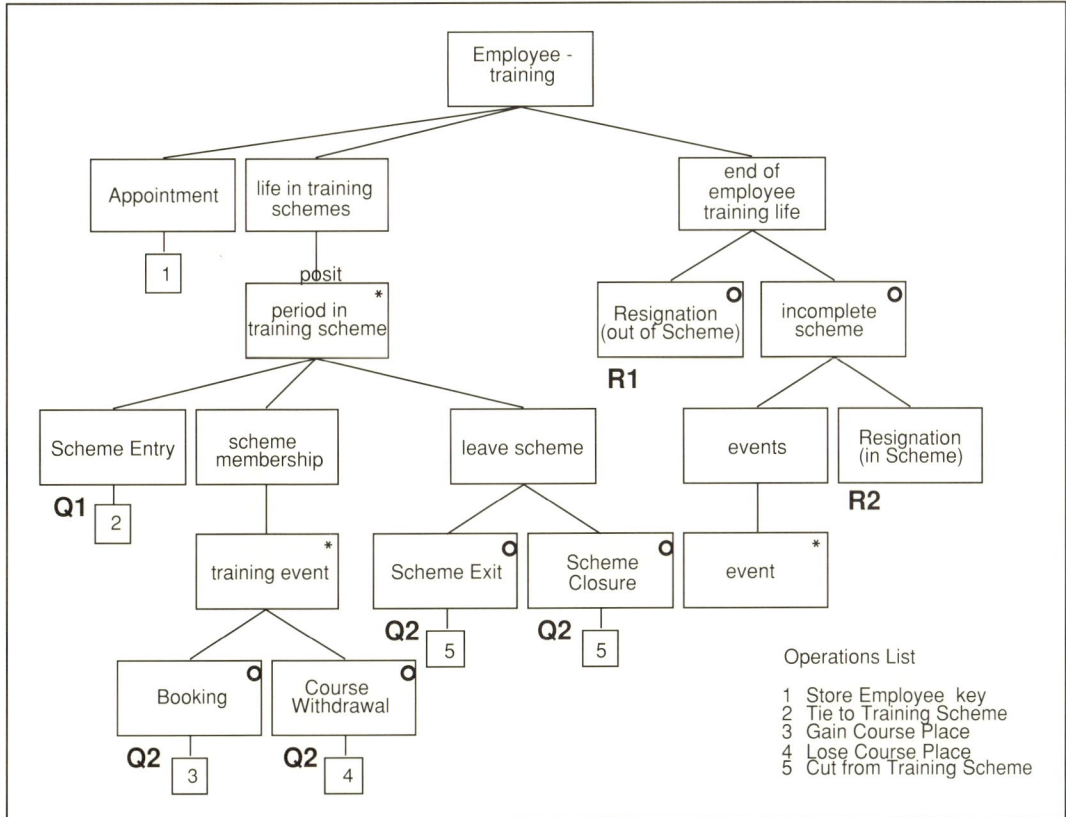

Figure 4.22: ELH for training aspect of employee

Note that the employee-training ELH uses the 'disciplined quit' convention, where:

- the 'posit' means 'stay unconditionally within the iterated component until a quit event is encountered'

- each quit means 'transfer context to the corresponding resume instead of processing this event'

- the 'iteration of event' structure before Resignation (in scheme) is a notational convention to remind us to deal with any side effects of quitting part-way through a sequence of events. It could be omitted without affecting the semantics of the ELH.

4.6 Aspects identified in analysis of parallel life histories

In ELH analysis we may find asynchronous cycles in the life of one entity type. In SSADM version 4 we would develop a parallel life structure. We could, however, model the parallel lives as two aspects. For example, Task in Projects-R-Us has different cycles for work done and for budget control, as shown in Figures 4.23 and 4.24.

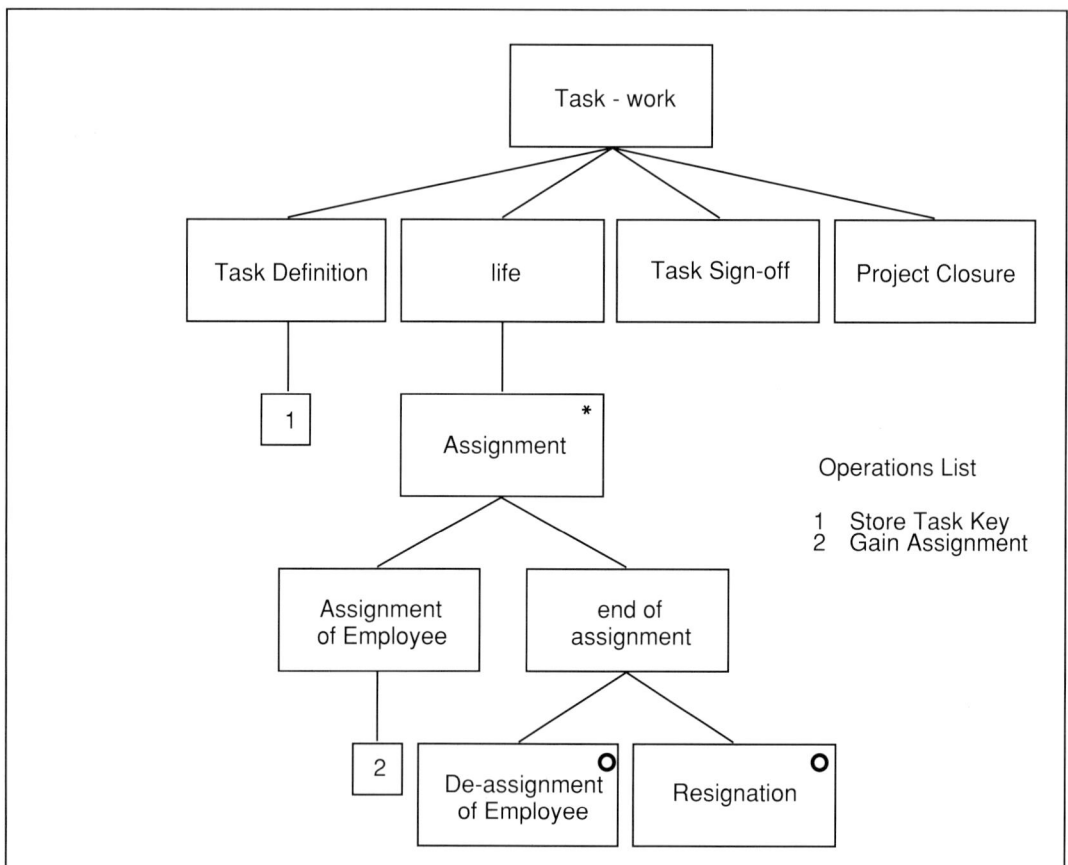

Figure 4.23: Work done leg of parallel life modelled as a separate ELH for work aspect of task

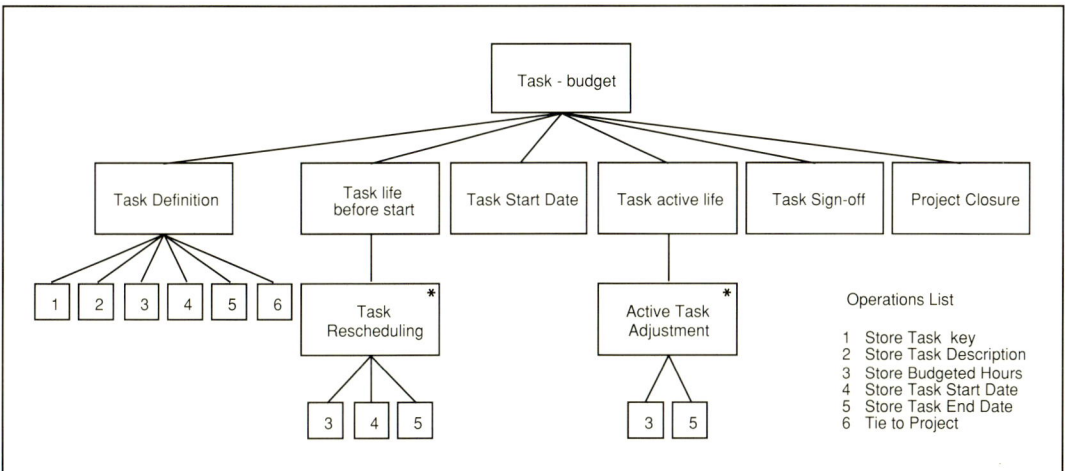

Figure 4.24: Budget leg of parallel life modelled as a separate ELH for budget aspect of task

This approach results in two simpler ELHs rather than one large one for Task. It also provides a further opportunity for partitioning the project control application, if required. See Figure 4.25. This might be done to allow work to progress in parallel, or to deliver the application in two phases.

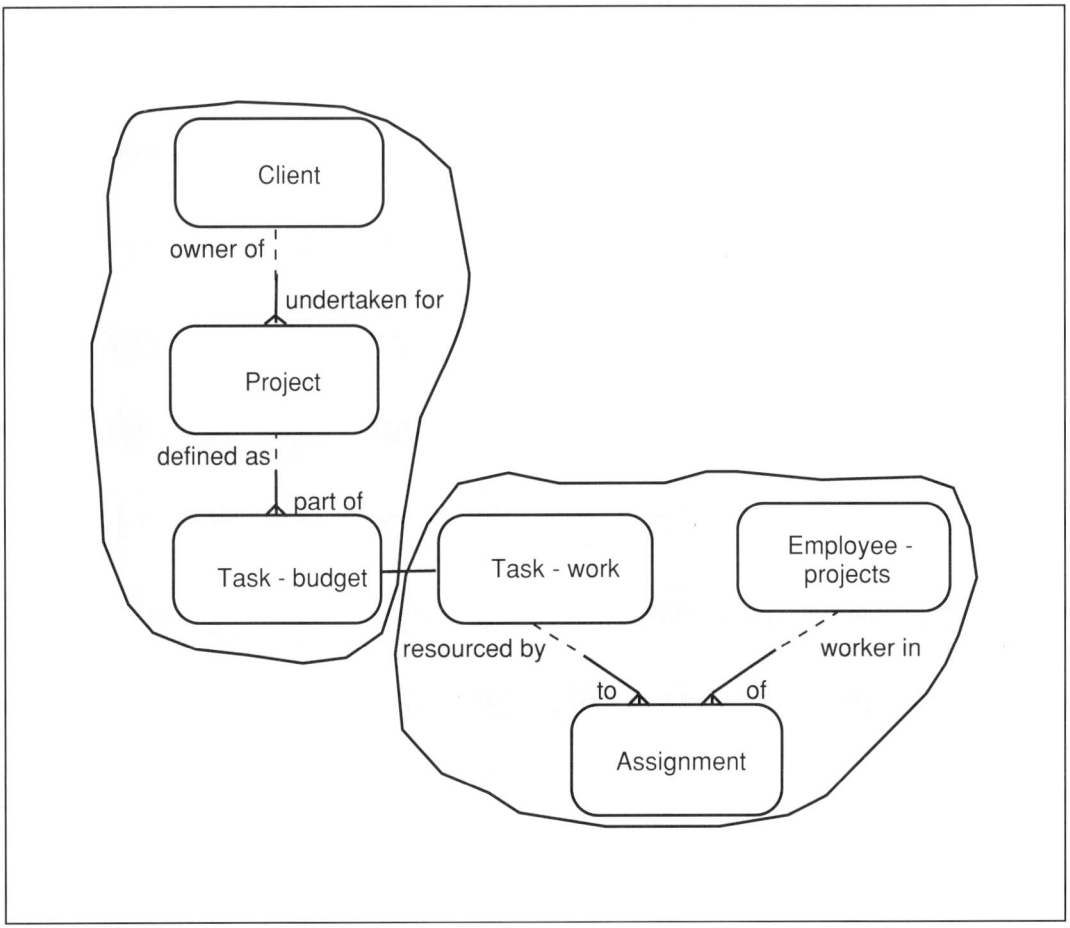

Figure 4.25: Possible further partitioning of Project Control application

In Chapter 5 the parallel aspects have been maintained, but included in the Project Control application.

5 Integrating separately-developed Conceptual Models

5.1 Summary

Conceptual Models of the applications, when implemented, will provide database update and enquiry processes that will be used by dialogues and batch processes in the External Design.

Many updates and enquiries are each wholly contained within one application - they are not affected by integration. Some update and enquiry processes span more than one application. It is these processes, rather than entire applications, that are integrated.

The approach for integration of Conceptual Models uses some relatively simple extensions of the SSADM techniques for developing update and enquiry process models.

Each update or enquiry process in an application has an entry point to the application's LDM, whose key is identified in the event data or enquiry trigger. If the update or enquiry spans more than one application, we have to identify which application has to be invoked by the event or enquiry, ie where in the entire system the process starts.

As we derive the process model (from the ECD or EAP) we add operations to invoke processes in other applications. These in their turn, may invoke further processes in other applications. Since the points of contact between applications are aspects, these operations are always simple invocations; there is no additional structure to be developed.

The approach for integration does not assume any particular implementation approach. There are several different implementation techniques, including subroutine calls, linkage of separately-compiled modules and client/server calls. Communication between applications may be local or remote.

5.2 Event processes within a single application

The guidelines for partitioning the Conceptual Model should lead to fairly self-contained project areas. Many processes in the Conceptual Model should be contained within one application.

For example, Task Definition in Projects-R-Us is completely contained within the project control application. See Figures 5.1 and 5.2.

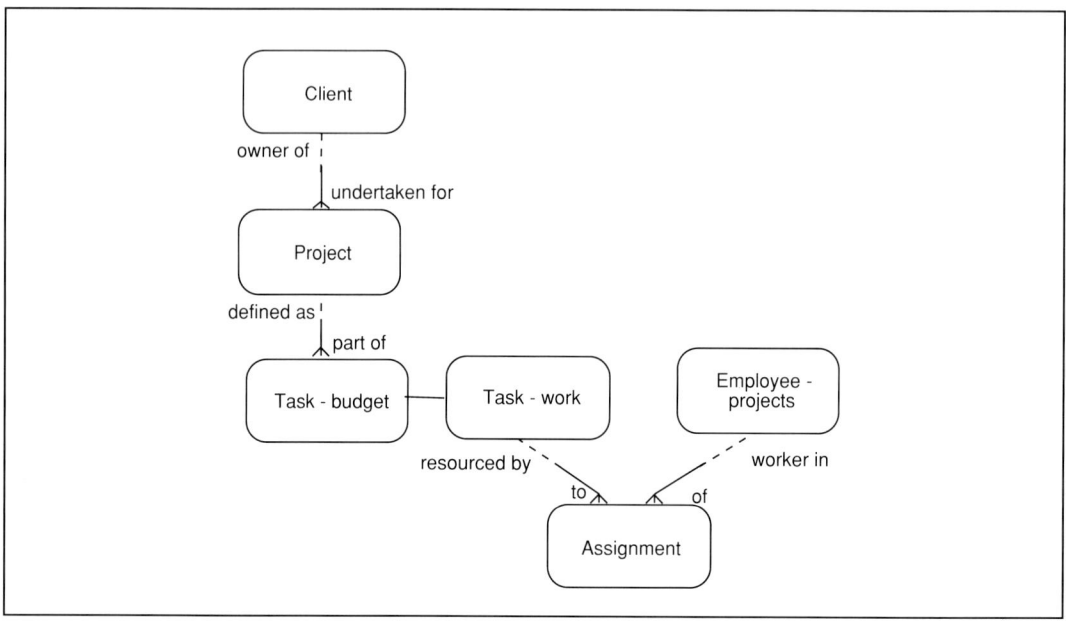

Figure 5.1: LDM for project control application

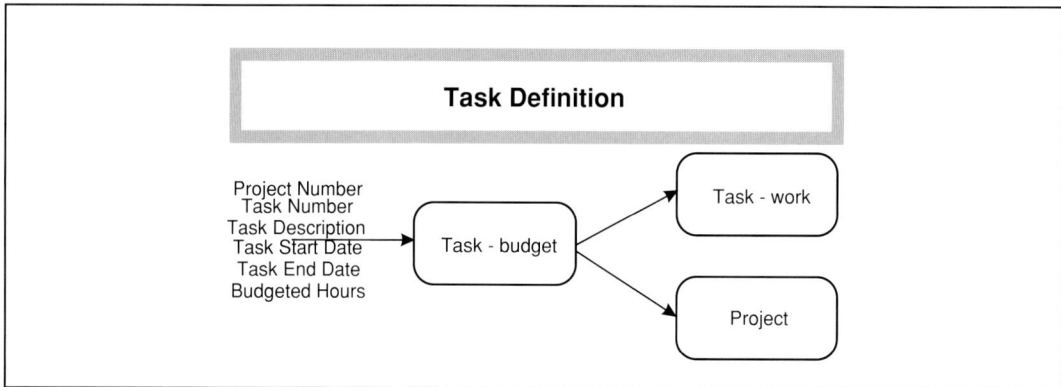

Figure 5.2: Task Definition is contained within the project control application

Chapter 5
Integrating separately-developed Conceptual Models

5.3 Read-only access across applications

When creating ECDs we have to include any entities that are needed for reference but not updated (so that the event does not occur in their ELHs).

Sometimes, what is needed is access to attributes of the basic aspect of a shared entity. If the basic aspect is outside the event's application (ie on a separate server, or merged into another application), the UPM has to invoke an enquiry.

For example, in Projects-R-Us: one week before a course presentation is scheduled, joining instructions are sent out if there are places booked; the presentation is cancelled if there are no bookings. See Figure 5.3.

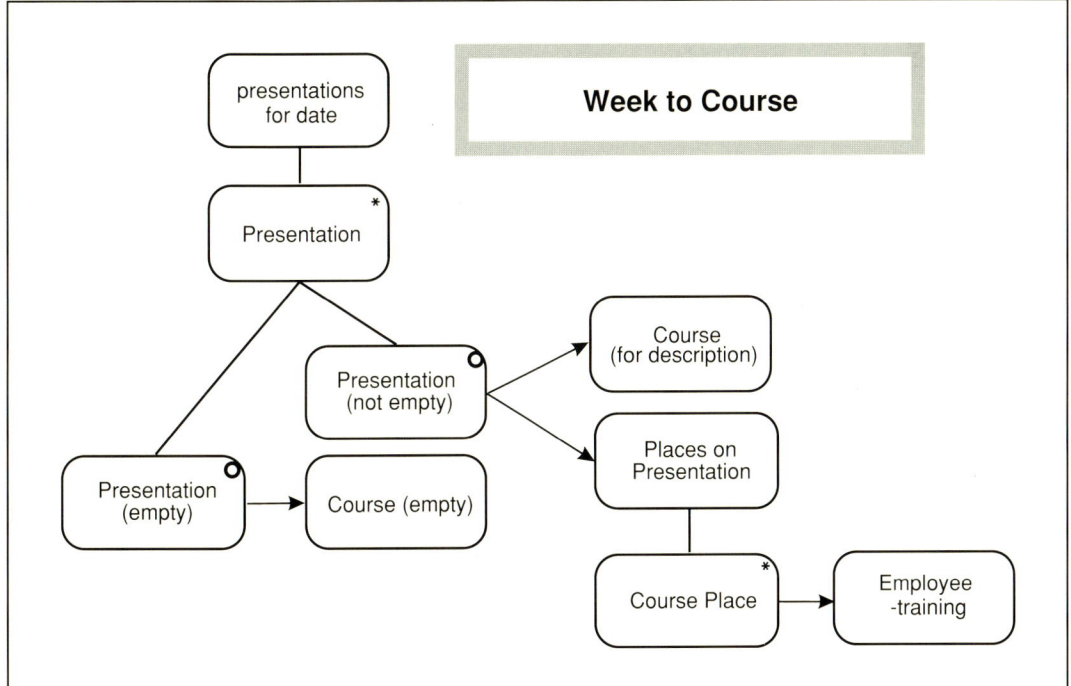

Figure 5.3: Week to Course ECD

67

Employee Name and Department Number are needed for joining instructions, but they are in the shared server. We need an enquiry to obtain them. This is likely to be a reusable enquiry. If so, it will be invoked by its own independent enquiry name; there would not be a specific enquiry called 'Week to Course - employee & dept'. See Figure 5.4.

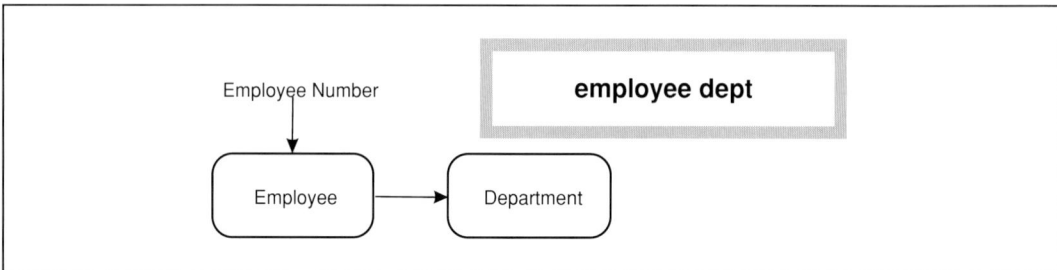

Figure 5.4: Employee department ECD

In the UPM for Week to Course we need to include an operation to invoke the enquiry as shown in Figure 5.5.

Chapter 5
Integrating separately-developed Conceptual Models

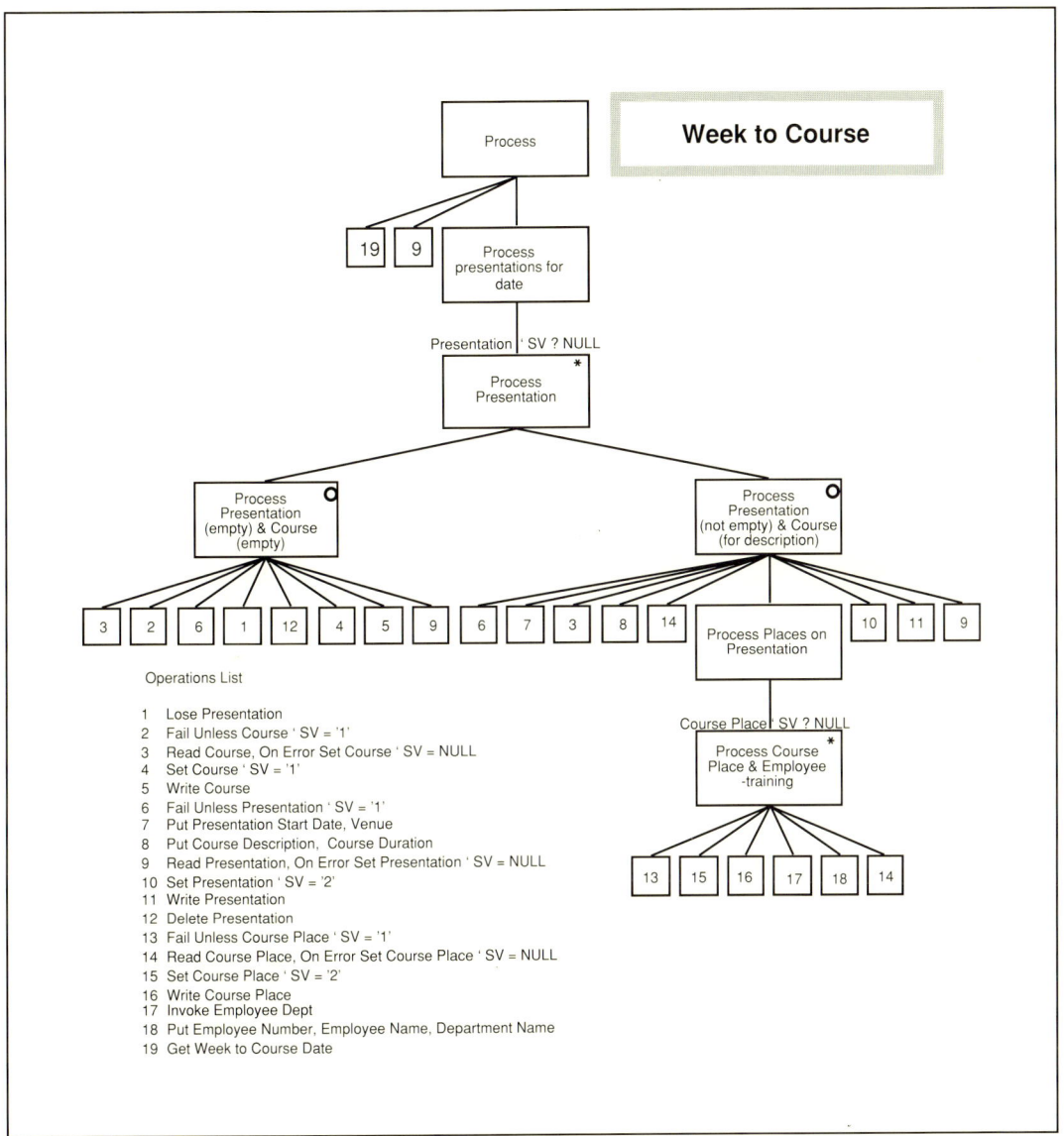

Figure 5.5: Week to Course UPM - note operation 17

5.4 Event processes spanning more than one application

Some event processes span more than one application; for example, births and deaths of shared entities. Project Closure in Projects-R-Us spans the project control and time recording applications, as shown in Figures 5.6 and 5.7.

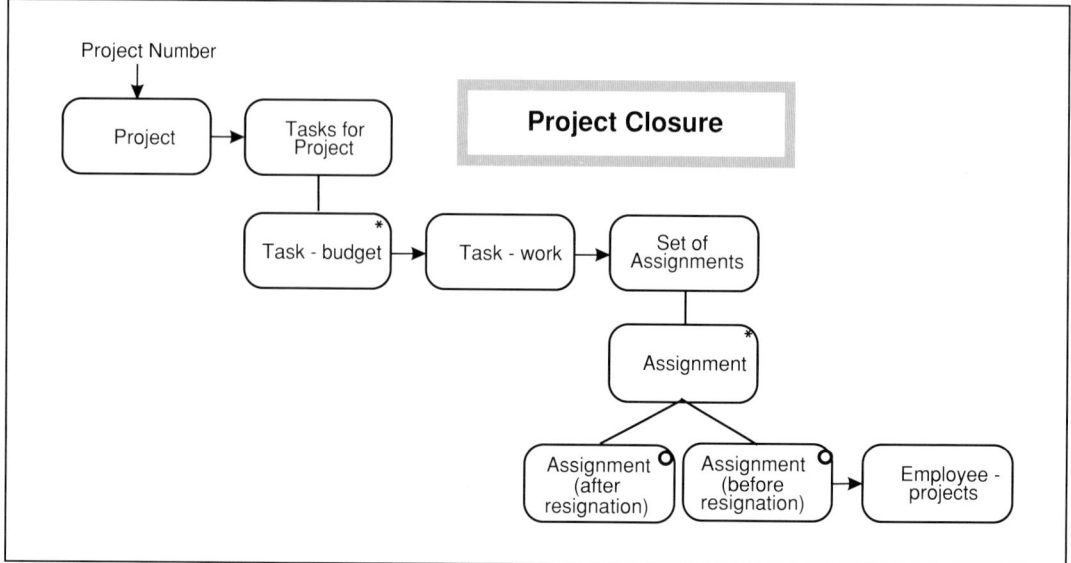

Figure 5.6: Project Closure ECD - project control fragment

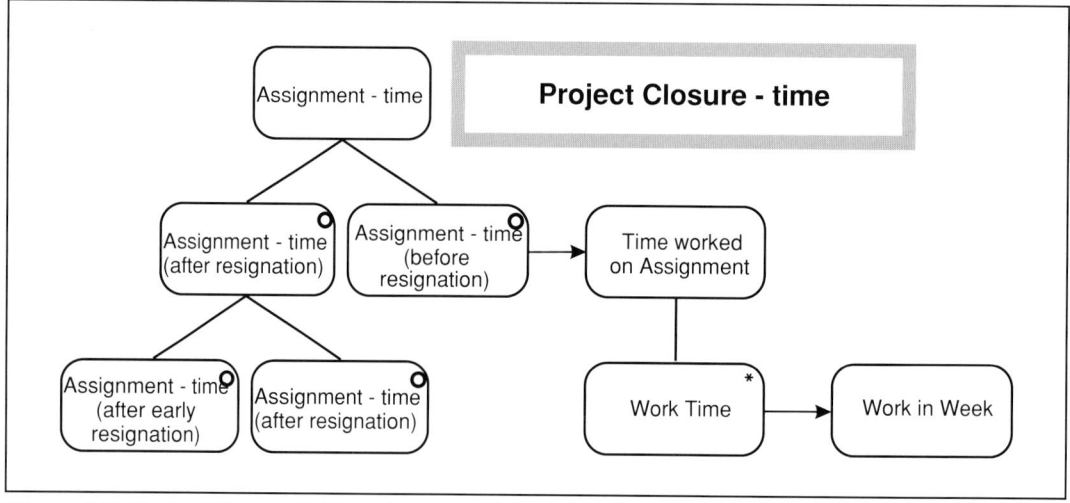

Figure 5.7: Project Closure ECD - time recording fragment

The entry point is Project. The link between the two ECDs is the one-to-one correspondence between Assignment in the project control application and Assignment-time in the time recording application. To integrate the two processes we need to allocate a new operation to Assignment when creating the UPM in the project control application: 'invoke Project Closure - time and fail if it fails'. See Figure 5.8.

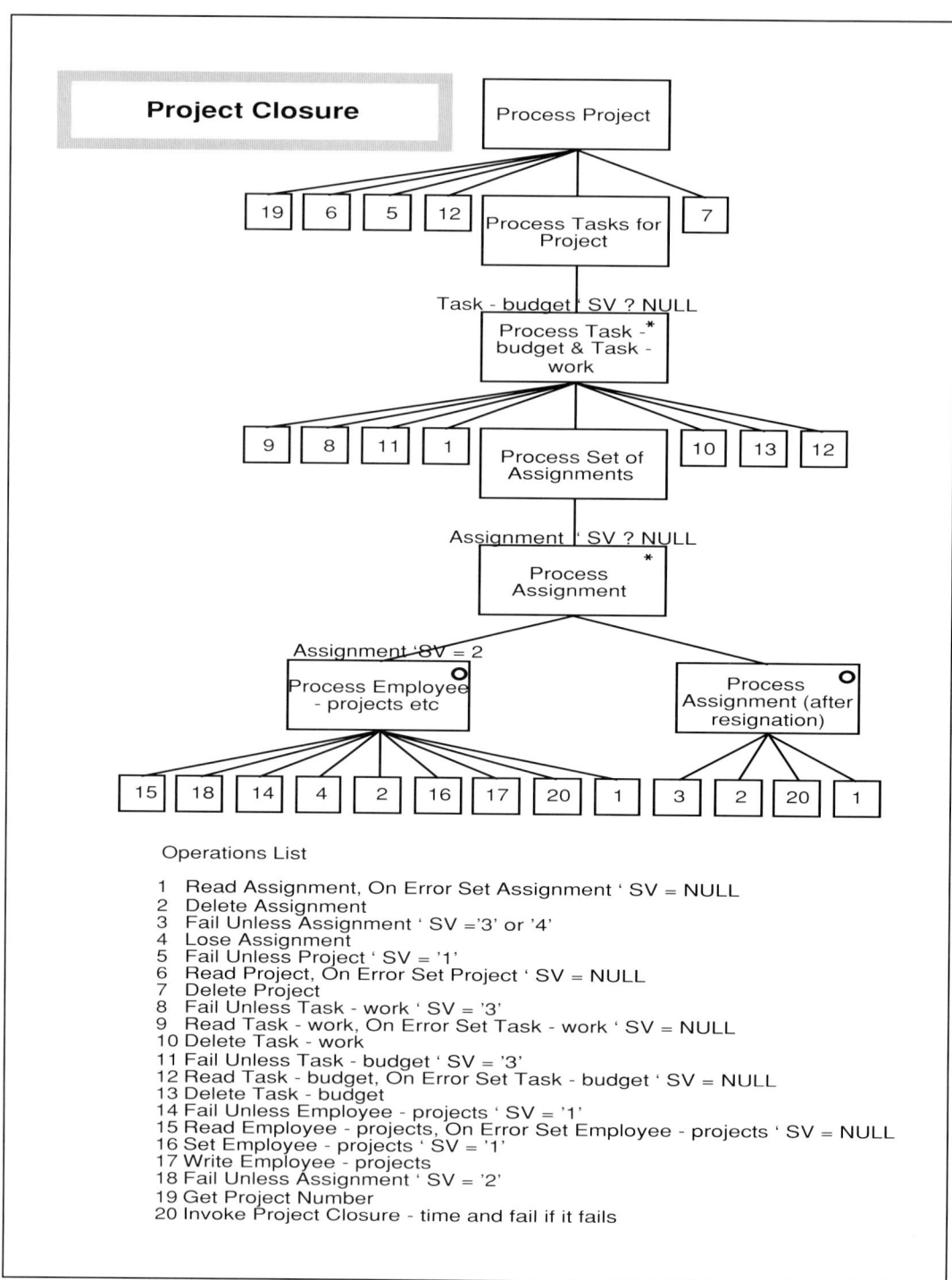

Figure 5.8: Project Closure UPM in project control application - note operation 20

The UPM for Project Closure in the time recording application is created in the usual way. See Figure 5.9.

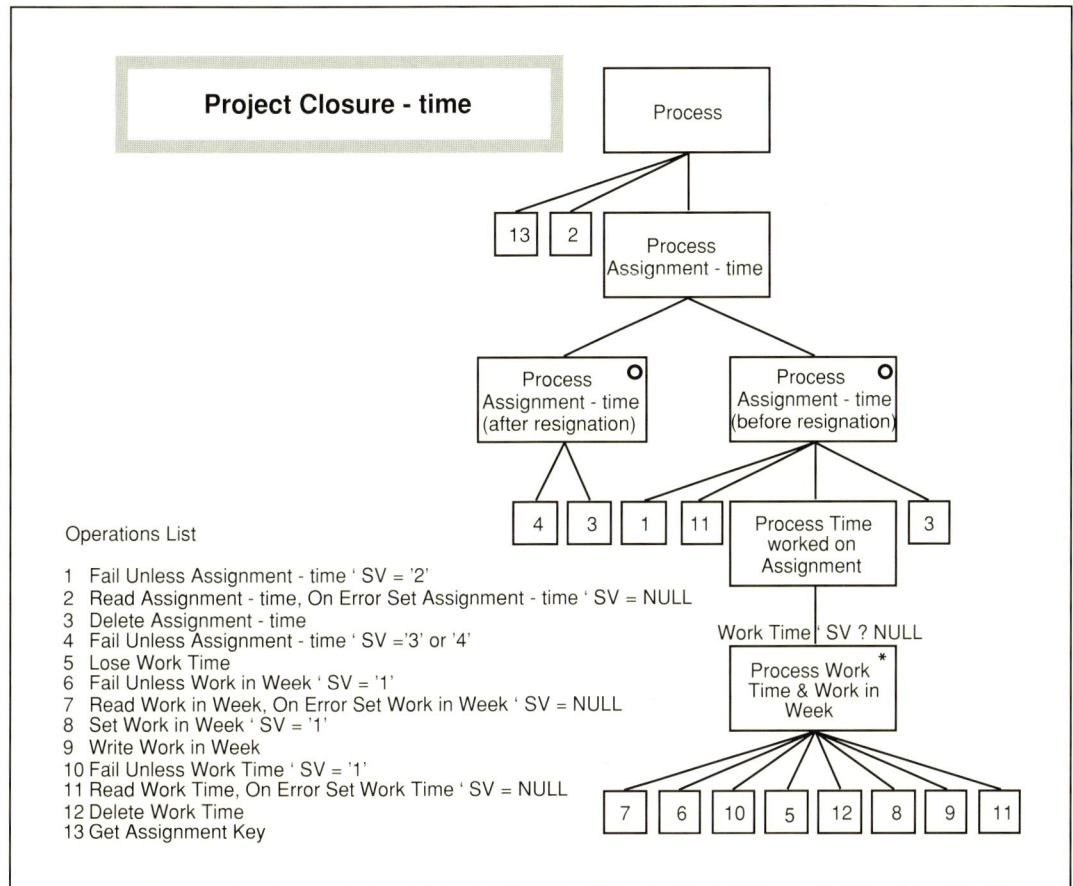

Figure 5.9: *Project Closure UPM in time recording application*

The process shown in Figure 5.9 will be invoked for each assignment in the project. Since Assignment's key is hierarchical (under Project and Task) it would be possible to iterate this process - 'all assignments for all tasks in a project' - and invoke it once from the project control application. We shall return to this in Chapter 7 as a possible optimisation.

5.5 Ambiguous correspondences

In the previous example, Project Closure, integration between project control and time recording was simple because there was only one point of correspondence - Assignment.

Where there are correspondences in the same event process between aspects of several different entities, there may be 'loops' of relationships. We have to ensure that the UPM does not make incorrect accesses to the same entity.

ECDs for LDM loops

The problem is not specific to integration of separate applications. It can happen within a single application. For example, there is a loop in the LDM for the training application in Projects-R-Us, as shown in Figure 5.10.

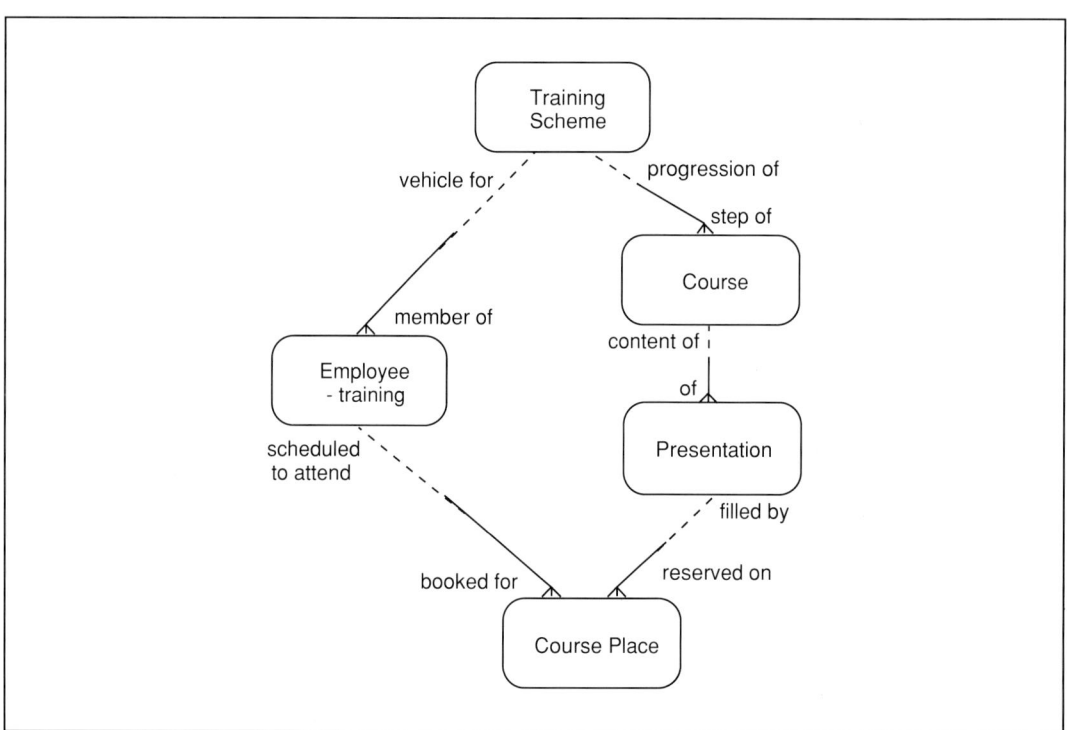

Figure 5.10: Loop in the LDM of the training application

The ECD for an event that affects all entities in the loop cannot use all relationships in the loop.

For example, when a training scheme is closed, all employees in it leave the scheme and any course places booked for them are cancelled. All current and future presentations of courses in the scheme are cancelled along with all their places.

In the IT system, Training Scheme, its Courses and completed Presentations and Course Places are to be retained as history; cancelled Presentations and Course Places are to be deleted.

Ignore some relationships

What correspondence(s) should be drawn with course place in the ECD? There is a one-to-many relationship between Employee and Course Place ('employee may be scheduled to attend one or more course places'), and another between Presentation and Course Place ('presentation may be filled by one or more course places'). One of these relationships must be ignored in creating ECD correspondences. Course Place cannot occur in two different iterations in one ECD.

If we omit the correspondence between Employee and Course Place the ECD is as shown in Figure 5.11.

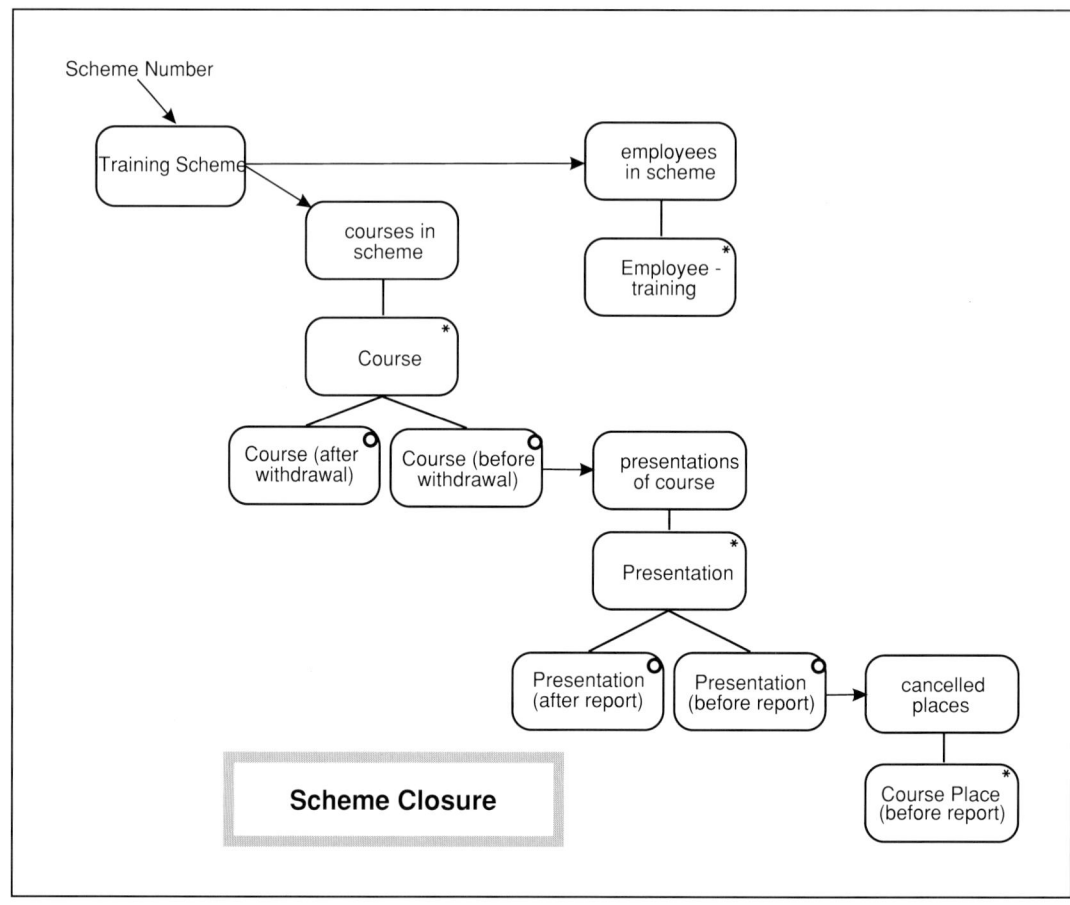

Figure 5.11: Scheme Closure ECD where correspondences between Employee and Course Place have been ignored

If we omit the correspondence between Presentation and Course Place the ECD is as shown in Figure 5.12.

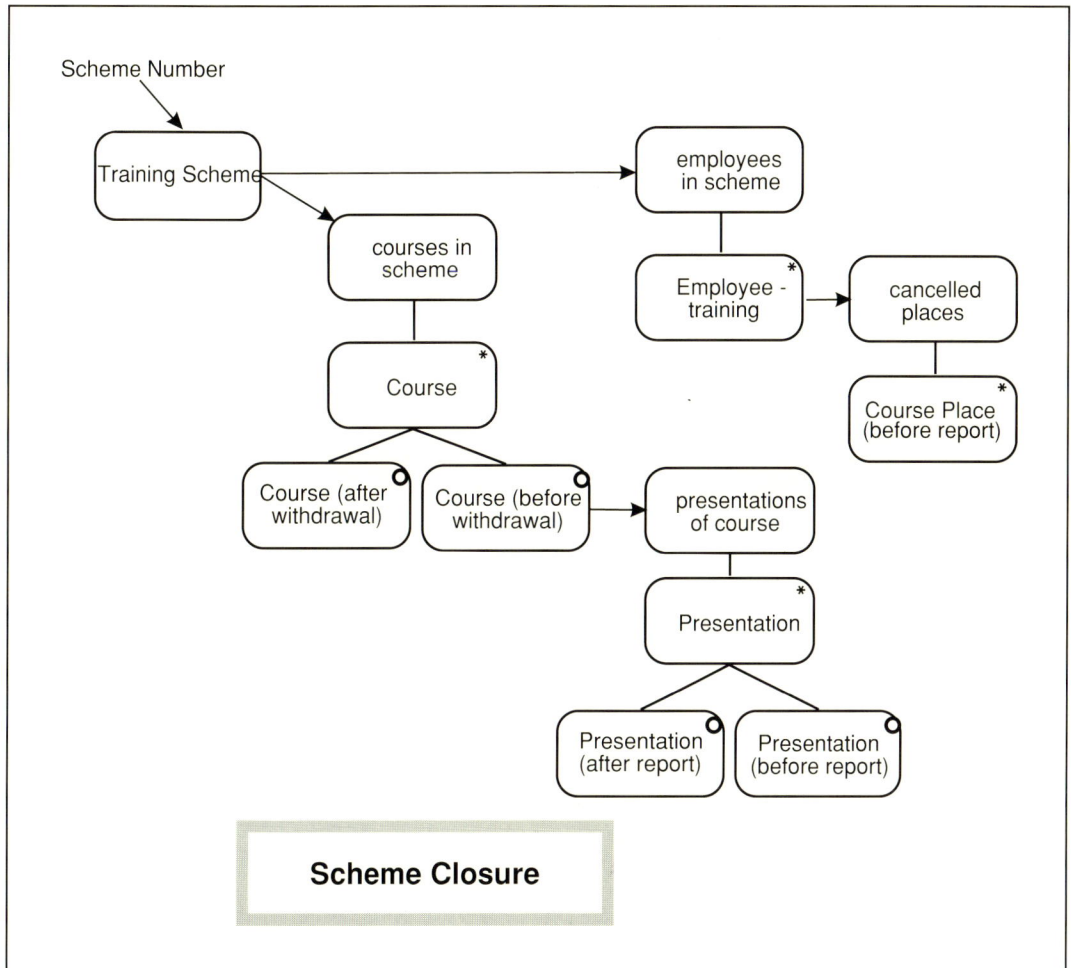

Figure 5.12: Scheme Closure ECD where correspondences between Presentation and Course Place have been ignored

The two ECDs are not equivalent. The ECD of Figure 5.11 will provide the correct UPM. It will cancel course places for all current and future presentations (ie those for which a report has not been received). It will not affect Course Places for Presentations with 'completed' status - they are to be kept as history until the scheme is removed.

The ECD of Figure 5.12 will produce a UPM that will attempt to cancel all course places for each employee in the scheme. Any historical Course Place will be in a state that is invalid for this event, and will cause the UPM to fail.

Loops between applications

The important point about this is that we have to take care to identify loops, and then identify which relationships should be ignored - so that the resulting ECD will provide the correct UPM.

We have to do this whether a loop is within a single application, or spans several applications, although it may be more difficult to recognise loops that span several applications.

Another example - Employee Resignation

In Projects-R-Us there are two loops involving Employee Resignation; one for work time and one for training time as shown in Figure 5.13.

Employee Resignation affects the entities in both loops. The entities that can be accessed from more than one direction are Work Time and Training Time, so in the ECD for employee resignation we need to ignore one relationship for each of them.

When an employee resigns, their Assignments are to be retained for project history (Assignment-time contains a summary of hours worked); Employee (all aspects) and the rest of its history are to be deleted.

We need to use the relationship 'assignment-time may be consumed by one or more work times', because Assignment-time will remain and has to lose its set of Work Times. But we could omit either of Training Time's relationships and obtain a valid ECD - all instances of Course Place (all aspects), Work in Week, Work Time and Training Time are to be deleted, however they are accessed.

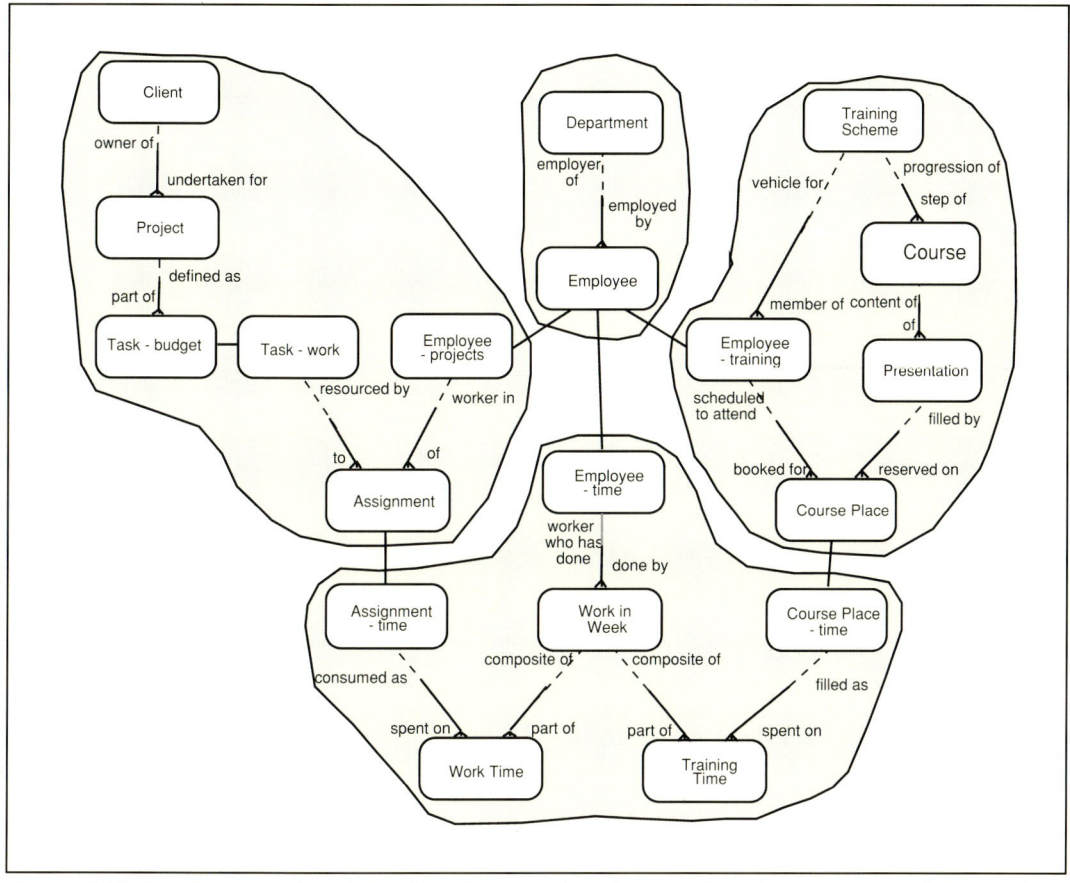

Figure 5.13: Work time and training time loops for Employee resignation in Projects-R-Us LDM

Fragmented ECD

In drawing ECD correspondences for Employee Resignation in the time recording application, we ignore the relationships:

- 'work in week may be a composite of one or more work times'; we need the alternative, 'assignment-time may be consumed by one or more work times', to obtain a valid ECD

- 'work in week may be a composite of one or more training times' (arbitrarily selected).

This causes Employee Resignation to be fragmented into three partial ECDs, as shown in Figure 5.14, and results in three UPMs.

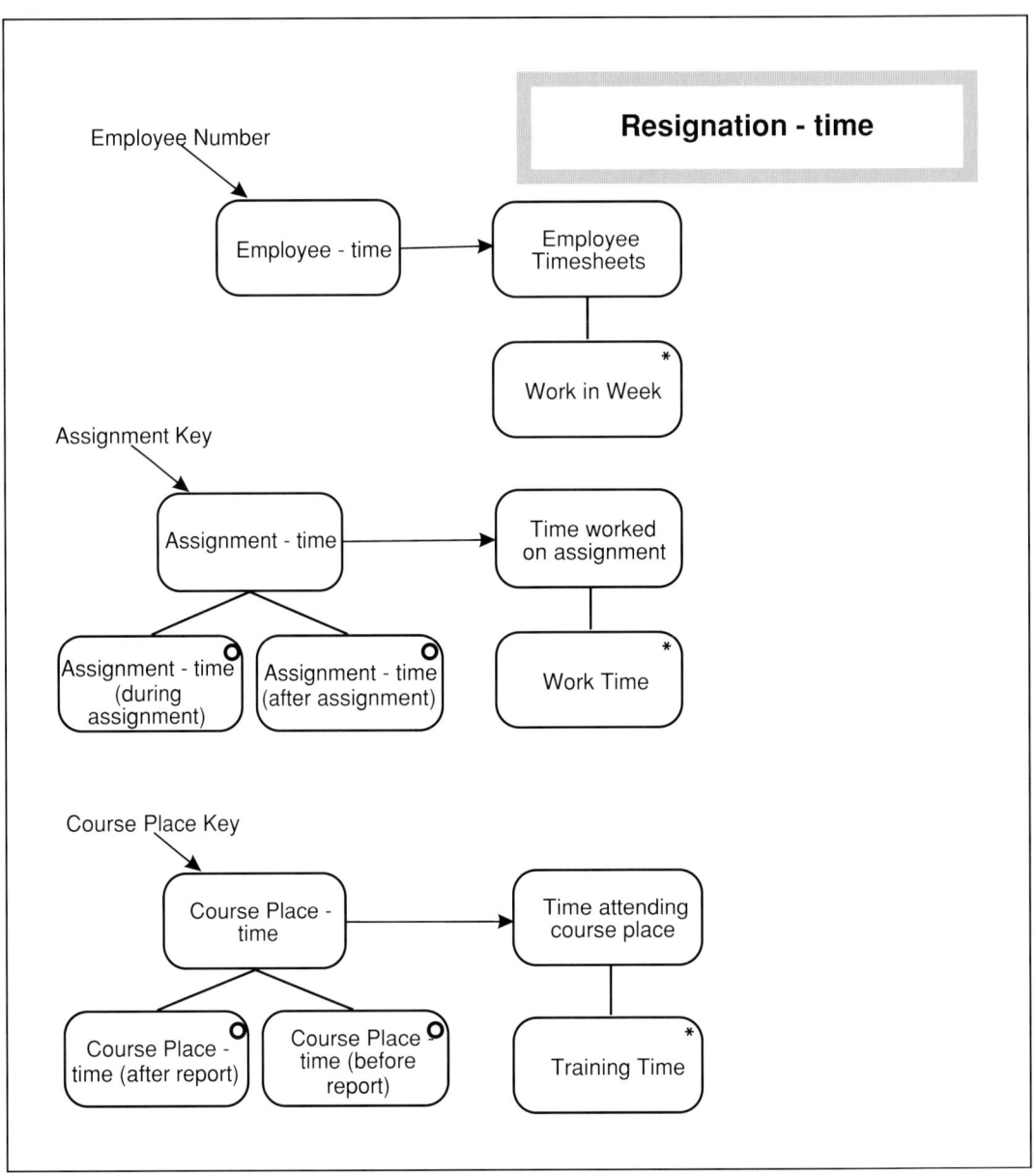

Figure 5.14: Partial ECDs for Employee Resignation in time recording application

Resignation affects Employee in all applications, including the shared server. The shared server's UPM will invoke three further UPMs - for the aspects of employee in time recording, project control and training management. These invocations are noted on the ECD for the shared server, as shown in Figure 5.15.

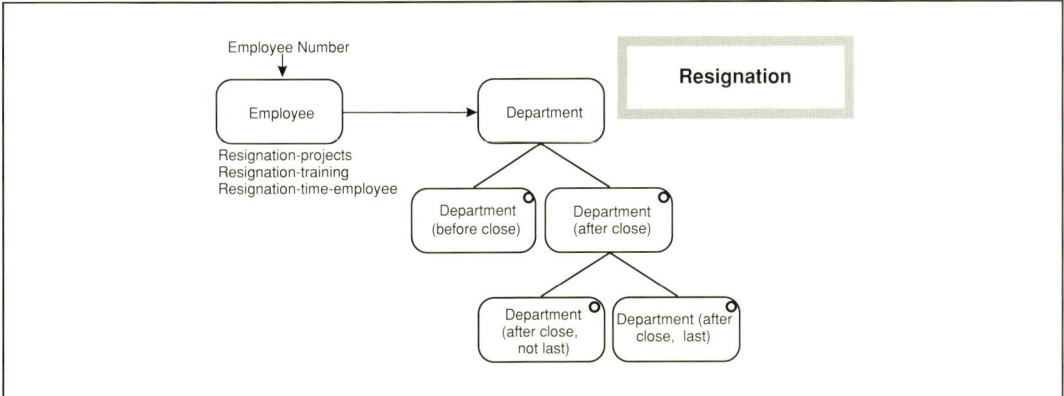

Figure 5.15: Employee Resignation ECD for shared server with additional invocations noted under Employee

The UPM for the shared server is as shown in Figure 5.16.

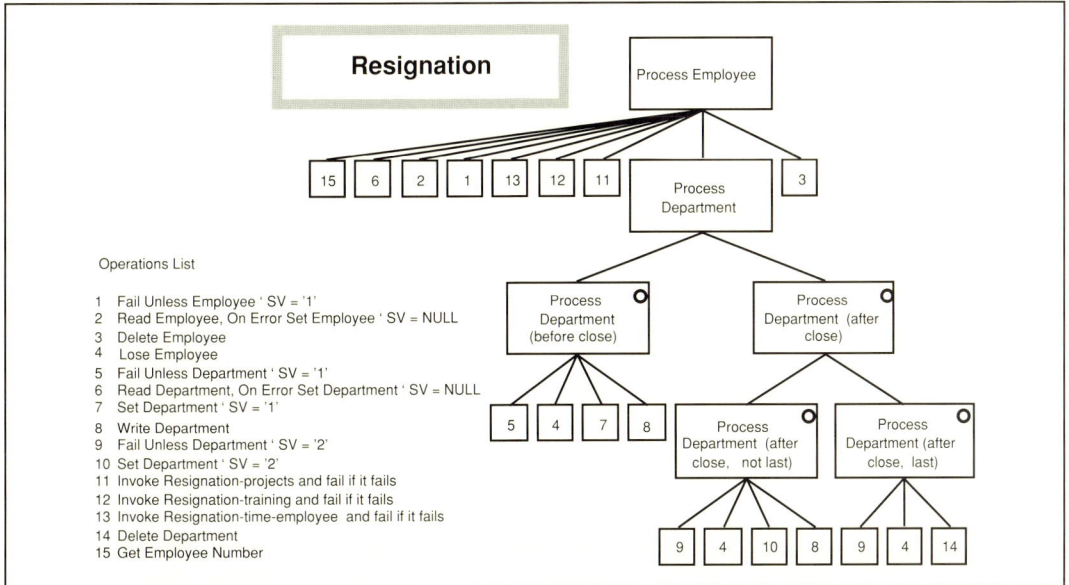

Figure 5.16: Employee Resignation UPM for shared server with additional invocations at operations 11, 12 and 13

The time recording UPM invoked by the shared server UPM for Resignation is illustrated in Figure 5.17. It is derived from the ECD fragment triggered by Employee Number, shown in Figure 5.14.

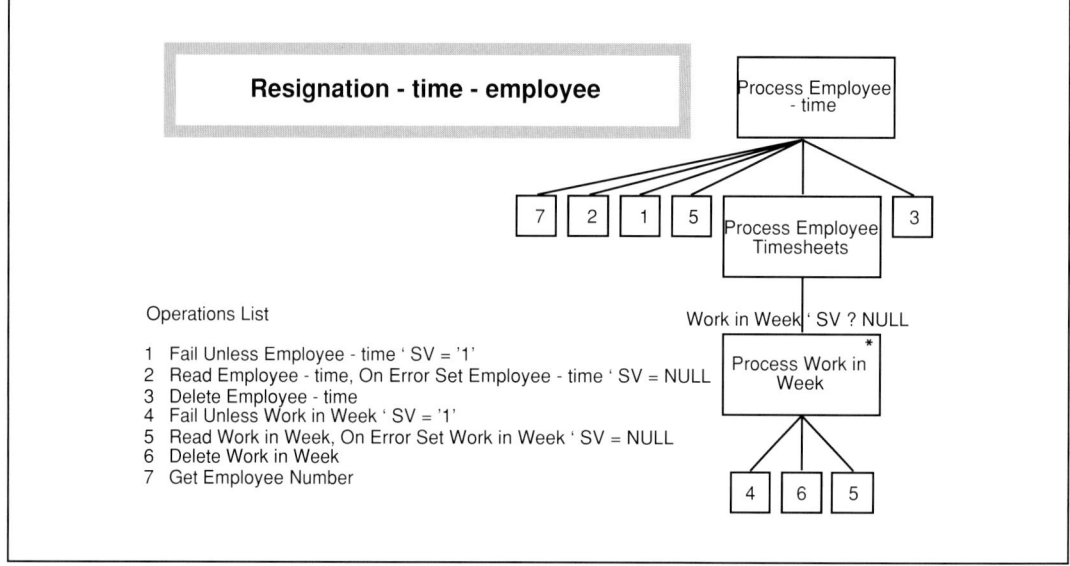

Figure 5.17: Employee Resignation UPM for time recording application

The ECD for resignation in the project control application is as shown in Figure 5.18.

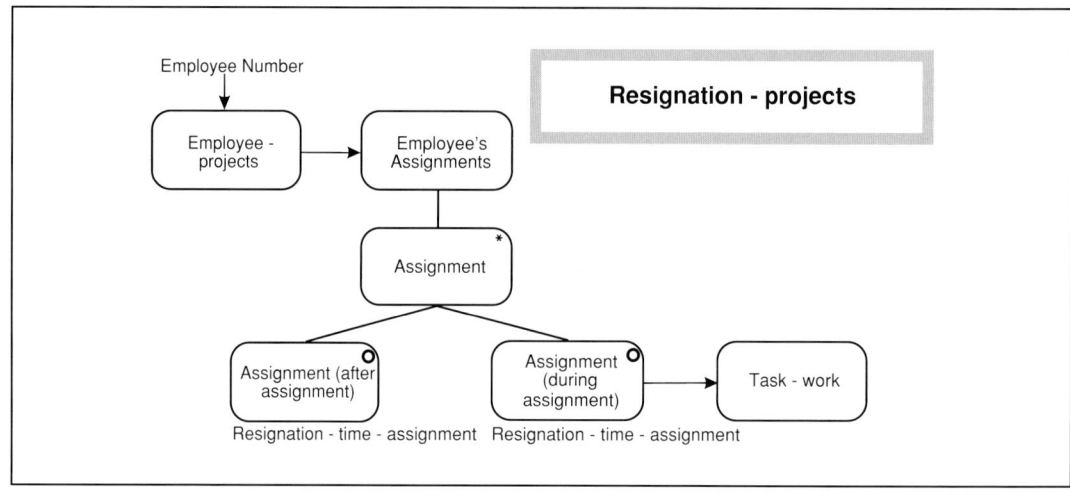

Figure 5.18: Employee Resignation ECD for project control application

The project control UPM for Resignation (Figure 5.19) derived from this ECD (Figure 5.18) will be invoked by the basic Resignation process (Figure 5.16). The project control UPM will then invoke a UPM (Figure 5.20) derived from the ECD fragment triggered by Assignment Key in the time recording application (Figure 5.14).

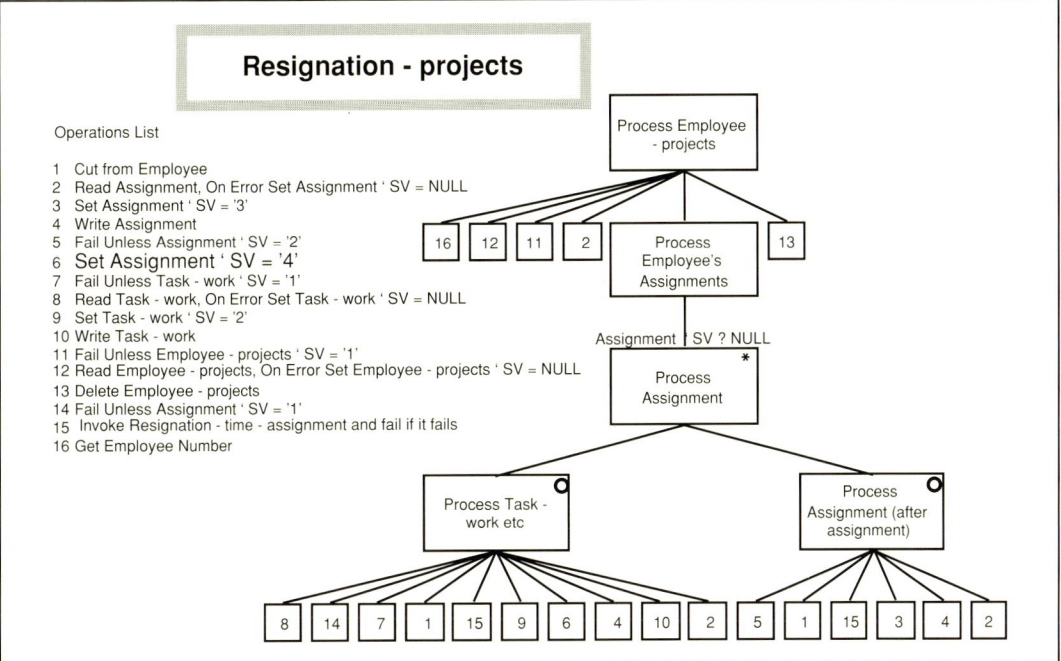

Figure 5.19: Employee Resignation UPM for project control application

The time recording UPM invoked by the project control UPM is as shown in Figure 5.20.

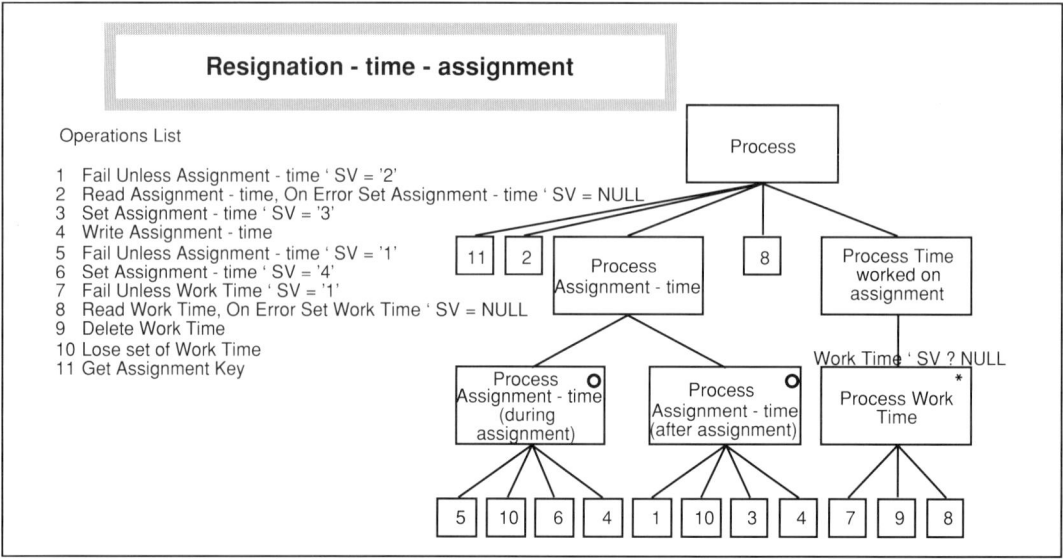

Figure 5.20: *Employee Resignation UPM for time recording application, invoked from project control UPM*

The Resignation ECD in the training application is as shown in Figure 5.21.

The UPM derived from this will be invoked by the basic Resignation process (Figure 5.16). It will then invoke a UPM in the time recording application, derived from the ECD fragment triggered by Course Place Key shown in Figure 5.14.

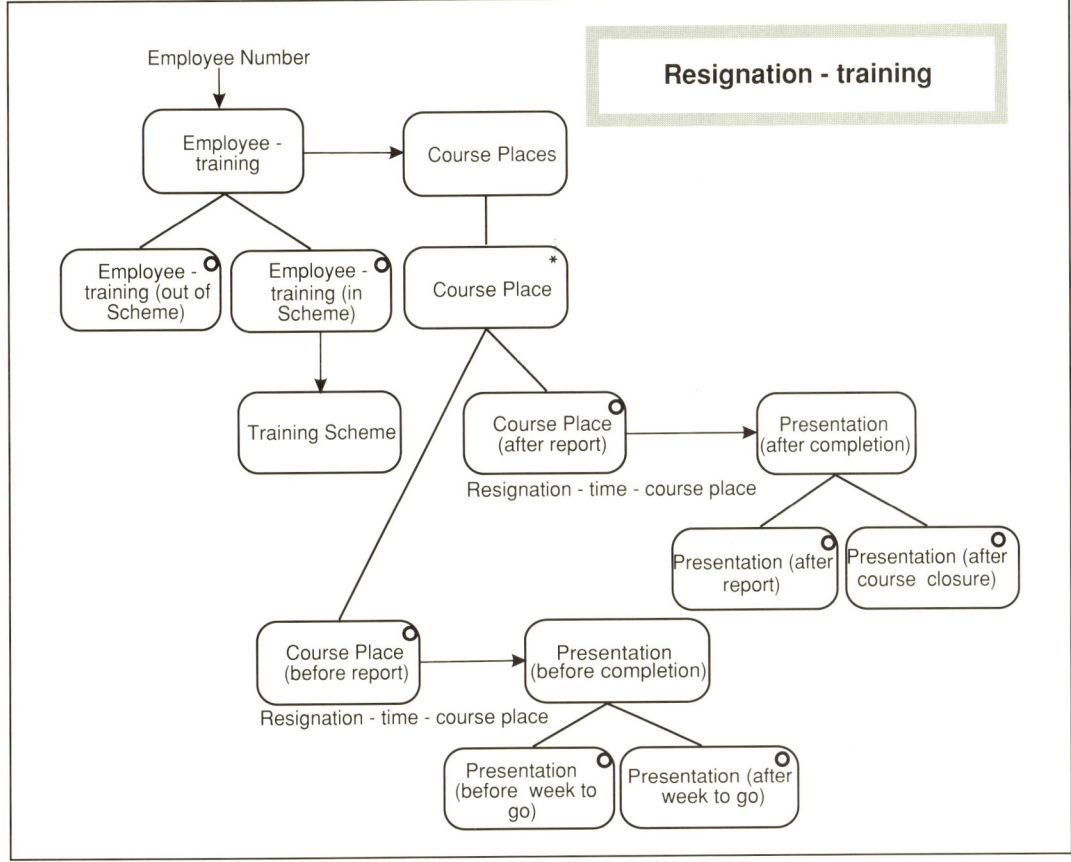

Figure 5.21: Employee Resignation ECD for training application

5.6 Reusable Update Processes	In general, when creating ECDs, it is often difficult to see processes that are similar or identical. When applications are partitioned and processing is localised it may be easier.

For example, in the time recording application in Projects-R-Us, the effects of Course Withdrawal and Training Scheme Closure are identical in structure. See Figures 5.22 and 5.23.

When operations are added and UPMs are created, they turn out to be identical in content. |

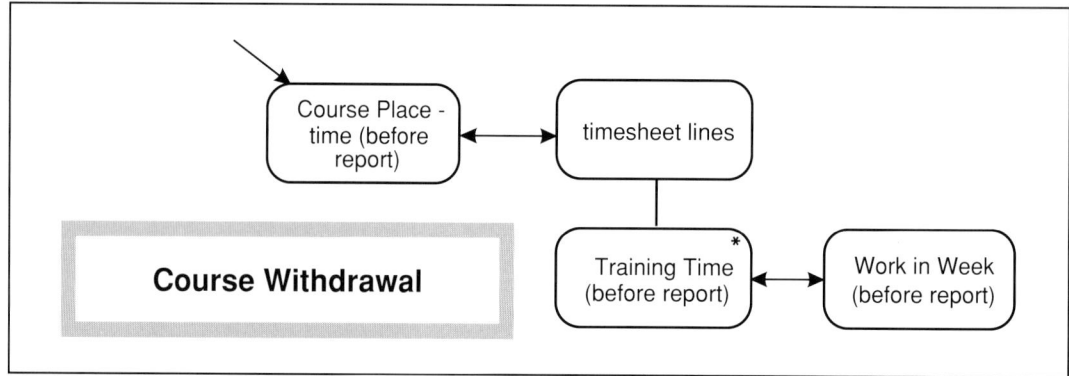

Figure 5.22: Course Withdrawal ECD in time recording application

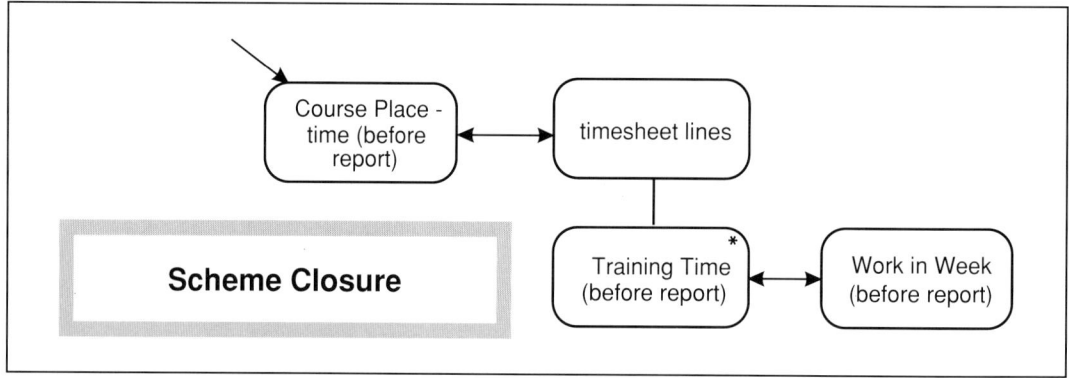

Figure 5.23: Training Scheme Closure ECD in time recording application

Super-events   However, identifying reusable components by inspection when creating ECDs, though useful, is not wholly reliable. The *ISE Library Volume: Reuse in SSADM using OO* describes an extension to ELH analysis, called super-events, that provides a more systematic way of identifying this kind of reusability.

Effects of deletion strategy   The strategy for history and deletion will often restrict the reusability of processes. For example, Assignment-time can be terminated in two ways:

- De-assignment: all history is retained

- Resignation: historical detail for the employee (Work in Week and Work Time) is deleted. Hours worked are held as a summary in Assignment-time

Chapter 5
Integrating separately-developed Conceptual Models

5.7 **Implementation of Conceptual Models**

Update and enquiry processes are implemented as database processes that operate on the LDM. The mapping to the physical database is handled by the program-data interface and is discussed further in Chapter 7.

Process invocation

Invocation of one process by another can be implemented in a number of ways, including:

- the invoked process as a subroutine in the same compiled module as the invoking process

- linked, separately compiled modules; the calls may be local or remote

- the invoking process as client and the invoked process as server. (Note that some client/server vendors discourage this; they recommend a simple architecture of dialogue as client and database process as server).

This direct implementation approach, maintaining the LDM as the Conceptual Model's view of the database, is adequate for most processes. In a few cases, physical design issues will necessitate some distortion of the process structures or the communication between them; see Chapter 7.

Aspect birth

It may be the case that an aspect is 'not yet active'; for example, Employee-training for an employee who has not yet been assigned to a training scheme. In some physical designs, this could mean that the Employee-training database record does not yet exist: see Chapter 7.

Enquiry processes may need to distinguish valid and invalid reasons for failure to find a database record; eg for the Personal Training Schedule (which course presentations an employee is scheduled to attend):

- 'valid employee, not in any training scheme'

- 'unknown employee'.

6 External Design

6.1 Summary

External Design is a mapping of conceptual services on to user roles and interface technology. The major design components are functions, which invoke event and enquiry processes.

Functions provide support for business activities carried out by user roles. They will be implemented as dialogues or in a batch input/output subsystem.

The External Design interacts with the whole Conceptual Model, ie a function may use events and enquiries that operate on more than one application. However, the guidelines for partitioning the Conceptual Model (Chapter 4) tend to localise IT support for particular user roles within an application.

We deal with the External Design of the first application as a special case. In subsequent applications we look for:

- reuse of existing components in providing functions to new user roles

- extension of the support provided to existing user roles.

6.2 User roles

User roles can be specified at two levels: roles in the organisation and 'service users'.

A service user is a role seen from the IT system's view. Events and enquiries are packaged into functions; functions are grouped to support particular types of business activity, each carried out by a service user.

Roles in the organisation can be defined (in respect of use of the IT system) by grouping service user roles into job specifications. The Inland Revenue has extended this approach. Service users are specified within the IT system, but IR local office managers configure the job specifications to suit their own staff. User interfaces are tailored to reflect the local mapping.

The guidelines for project partitioning lead to relatively easy identification of service users.

6.3 Functions in the 3-schema Specification Architecture

The basic building block of the External Design is the function. Service users are defined in terms of what functions they are permitted to invoke. Within the 3-schema Specification Architecture the role of a function is:

- to ensure that input from the user is syntactically correct

- to break user input down into event data and enquiry triggers; this may require the function to obtain data items not provided in the input, by calculation or look-up of reference data

- to provide an invocation structure (sequences, selections, iterations) for the events and enquiries used by the function

- to return output from events and enquiries to the user; this may involve sequencing, summary, calculation of derived data

- to diagnose and report semantic errors identified by event and enquiry processes.

Functions interact with the Conceptual Model as a whole. The partitioning of the Conceptual Model into separate applications should not, in principle, affect the specification of functions. A function invokes whatever events and enquiries it needs, regardless of which applications they are implemented in.

In practice, the guidelines for partitioning the Conceptual Model tend to localise the events and enquiries for a service user in a small number of applications.

If the project has been partitioned to support phased delivery, events and enquiries used by functions (or available to create new functions) are implemented at different times. Some functions and user menus will have to be updated as new events and enquiries are implemented.

6.4 External Design of the first application

External Design of the first application is very similar to External Design in a stand-alone project, except that:

- some services may be incomplete until data can be provided by later applications
- shared servers may also be needed.

Functions

For example, in Projects-R-Us, suppose that we choose project control to be the first application. It needs support from the employee server. The functions required by users in the project control application are listed in Figure 6.1.

```
PROJECT CONTROL
```

User Role	Function	UPM/EPM	
Client Support	Start New Client	Contract Agreement	U
	Change Client details	Client Address Change	U
		Client Name Change	U
	Terminate Client	Client Withdrawal	U
Project Planner	Start New Project	Project Opening	U
		Task Definition	U
	Add Tasks to Project	Task Definition	U
	Change Task Details	Project Tasks	E
		Task Rescheduling	U
		Active Task Adjustment	U
	Terminate Project	Project Closure	U
Project Manager	Assign Employee	Employee Commitments	E
		Assignment of Employee	U
		Personal Work Schedule	E
	Change Assignment details	Employee Commitments	E
		Assignment Rebudgeting	U
		Assignment Rescheduling	U
		Personal Work Schedule	E
	Terminate Assignment	De-assignment of Employee	U
	Sign-off Task	Task Sign-off	U
	Initiate Billing	Work Done in Week	E
System-initiated	Change Task Status	Task Start Date	U

Figure 6.1: Project Control functions

The functions required by users in the employee server application are listed in Figure 6.2.

```
-----------------------------------------------------------------
EMPLOYEE SERVER
User Role         Function                   UPM/EPM
-----------------------------------------------------------------
```

User Role	Function	UPM/EPM	
Personnel	Open New Department	Department Opening	U
	Close Department	Department Closure	U
	Start Employee	Appointment	U
	Change Employee details	Transfer	U
		Name Change	U
		Seniority Change	U
	Terminate Employee	Resignation	U
		Personal Work Schedule	E
		Personal Training Schedule	E

Figure 6.2: Employee server functions

Missing services

We have to identify services that are needed by users of the first application but will be provided by other applications.

In the project control application in Projects-R-Us there are two:

- until the training application is delivered, only project commitments of employees can be seen when allocating them to tasks

- until the time recording application is delivered, work done on tasks cannot be seen.

We have two concerns: to ensure compatibility between applications, and to specify stop-gap measures for the users while they are waiting for subsequent applications to be delivered.

Chapter 6
External Design

Compatibility

We need to specify what data is to be returned from the other applications - data items for a training commitment, work done on an assignment - and ensure that we design output formats that will accommodate them as well as the output delivered by the first application.

We also need to incorporate 'stubs' into the External Design to display messages that training commitments and work done on assignments are not yet implemented. Figure 6.3 illustrates a possible format for employee commitments. It would not be reasonable to display the full format, apparently indicating that no employee had any training commitment, and no work had been done on any assignment, without these messages.

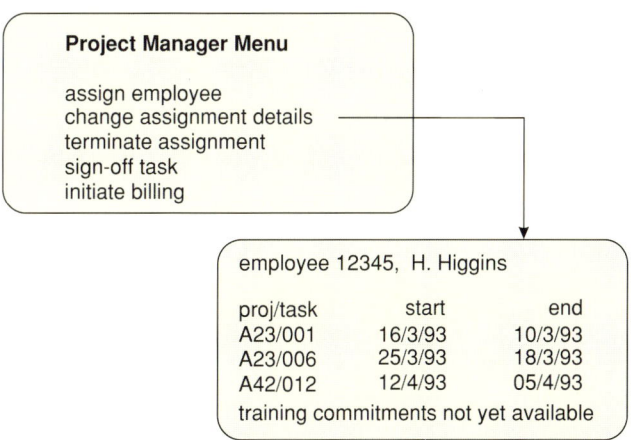

Figure 6.3: Possible format in External Design for Employee Commitment

Stop-gap measures

User instructions for the first application may have to provide some guidance on what to do in the absence of other applications. For example, if projects are running, Projects-R-Us presumably has to bill its clients, even if the time recording application has not yet been delivered. Is it possible to deliver the required data to the user's workstation from some existing IT system? If

93

it cannot be delivered in the required form, can it be loaded into, say, a spreadsheet so that the user can do the calculations?

Such guidance may not be necessary. For example, training (or formal management of training) may be a new business activity for Projects-R-Us, not supported until the training application is delivered.

| An optimisation | When enquiries correspond only at the entry point it is possible to define them as separate enquiries, and merge the results in the function. For example, an employee's name and department, project commitments, and training commitments could be retrieved separately and the results merged at the workstation before display.

In the Conceptual Model and External Design there is a minor trade-off. The three enquiry processes are independent of each other, and hence marginally simpler. The function gets two tables of employee commitments that it has to merge before sorting, rather than one table (that still has to be sorted). The merge has to be specified and coded for each type of workstation on which the function is to be implemented. None of these is very significant.

For enquiries with correspondences between aspects at lower levels than the entry point, merging separate sets of results at the function usually requires a batch process. For example, work done on a project could be derived by:

- retrieving the project, its tasks and assignments from the project control application

- retrieving all assignments for the project and their work time from the time-recording application

- matching the two sets of results on assignment id, and calculating the current state of each assignment from the group of work time details associated with the assignment.

Generally, it is more trouble than it is worth to do this kind of batch update in the function. It is simpler to integrate the two enquiries as described in Chapter 5 and build the output directly.

However, in a distributed system where applications are implemented at different sites there may be opportunities for improving performance by specifying separate partial enquiries. We shall return to these examples in the next chapter.

6.5 External Design of subsequent applications

As each subsequent application is developed, we have to be concerned with:

- External Design of functions provided to new user roles

- extending the External Design for users of already-installed applications to include new functions, or extensions of existing functions

- services developed in earlier applications that can be reused in the new application.

New user roles

We develop the External Design for new user roles in a new application in the same general way as for the first application; the only significant difference is the possibility of reuse of existing components.

In Projects-R-Us the next application is support for training. The new user roles and the functions they need are shown in Figure 6.4.

TRAINING MANAGEMENT			
User Role	Function	UPM/EPM	
Training Planner	Start New Scheme	Scheme Launch	U
		Course Approval	U
	Add Course to Scheme	Course Approval	U
	Change Course Director	Change of Course Director	U
	Add Presentations to Course	Receipt of Course	U
	Terminate Course	Course Withdrawal	U
		Personal Training Schedule	E
	Terminate Scheme	Scheme Closure	U
	Remove Scheme History	Scheme Removal	U
Personnel	Add Employee to Scheme	Scheme Content	E
		Scheme Entry	U
	Remove Employee from Scheme	Scheme Exit	U
Training Admin	Book Course Place	Course Place Availability	E
		Booking	U
		Personal Training Schedule	E
	Record Course Results	Course Report	U
	Cancel Course Place	Course Place Cancellation	U
	Training Progress Report	Training Progress	E
System-initiated	Joining Instructions	Week to Course	U
	Change Course Place Status	Presentation Start Date	U

Figure 6.4: Training functions

Existing user roles — We can extend the External Design for existing users by adding new functions and extending existing functions. New functions usually require additional menu options and, within dialogue design, navigation options to and from the new functions.

Extending existing functions is often done in the Conceptual Model, as described in Chapter 2. The impact on External Design may be minor; for example:

- extending the types of output displayed

- creating additional outputs , often to new user roles.

In Projects-R-Us training, the new functions for an existing user are for personnel:

- add employee to training scheme; inform training scheduler

- remove employee from training scheme.

Existing functions to be extended are:

- project control

    employee commitments now include course places; this replaces a stub (displaying 'training commitments not available' in the output format); it may need an additional line format for course place.

- personnel

    employee resignation - cancel course places and let training scheduler know; this does not affect the display to personnel staff, but results in an additional output.

Reuse

Much of the reusability in External Design is fairly mundane; for example:

- a strong application style guide supported by a library of components (eg log-on/off dialogue, menu template, help module, standard function keys, window and pop-up dialogue skeletons, buttons, icons etc) for each interface vehicle - text screens, MS-Windows, Motif, SQL-Forms, etc

- display attributes in the repository for data items - edit mask, name used on screen display, name used on reports (eg employee national insurance number: screen name N.I.No, report name N.I.No, format XX-999999-X)

- format for frequently-used groups of data items (eg basic employee data: employee number, employee name, date of birth, sex, department number).

These considerations are generally applicable. However, they are particularly important for applications that are to be integrated.

We should also look for reuse of processes in the Conceptual Model, and the External Design of their input and output. Reusable event processes were mentioned in Chapter 4. Because of the way we partition the Conceptual Model, events (or parts of events) are more likely to be reusable within applications than between them. Between applications, we are more likely to find reuse in enquiries.

For example, in Projects-R-Us:

- training schedulers need to know employee commitments; this uses the enquiry process developed for project controllers. If the training management interface is implemented on the same technology as that for project control, they can use the same External Design

- the general employee commitments enquiry invokes a process for training commitments. This process can be invoked in two other places:

  - to produce the employee's personal training schedule when a training scheduler has booked their course places

  - to inform the training scheduler of what course places have been cancelled when the personnel section inputs an employee resignation.

The output can be delivered as hard copy or EMail to the recipient, rather than to the dialogue that invoked it.

Chapter 6
External Design

Example - further application

The procedure for adding further applications is as described earlier in this section. The next application for Projects-R-Us is time recording. The new user role is time recording; the functions needed are as shown in Figure 6.5.

TIME RECORDING

User Role	Function	UPM/EPM	
Time Recording	Input Timesheets	Receipt of Timesheet	U
System-initiated	Late Timesheet	Missing Timesheets	E

Figure 6.5: Time recording functions

Existing user roles

Extensions to functions for existing user roles are:

- project control

    initiation of billing - work done to date on project available

    task rebudgeting - work done and elapsed time on task now available

- training scheduler

    evaluation of employee progress in scheme - attendance on course places now available.

7 Internal Design

7.1 Summary

First-cut design for integrated applications is similar to that for a free-standing application, except for minor changes to first-cut rules and PDI to take account of entity aspects.

If separately-developed applications are to be installed at the same site, design optimisation is similar to that for a free-standing application, with some additional guidance for dealing with aspects. If the applications are to be installed at different sites, we have to consider message traffic between sites.

7.2 First-cut Internal Design

First-cut database design

First-cut database design for integration of separately-developed applications is very similar to that for free-standing applications. The first-cut rules differ slightly to take account of multiple aspects of the same entity types.

Aspects

Where more than one aspect is modelled for an entity type:

- if aspects are to be implemented on the same computer and with the same DBMS, they are implemented as a single database table or record type. Each aspect becomes a view of the physical record, delivered by the PDI to update and enquiry processes

- if aspects are to be implemented on different computers or on different DBMSs, they are implemented as distinct database tables or record types. Instances are kept in synchronisation by using the same external identifier (eg employee number for employees in Projects-R-Us).

For further discussion on distribution of a partitioned LDM, see the *ISE Library Volume: Distributed Systems: Application Development*.

PDI for aspects If aspects are mapped on to a single physical table or record type, the PDI has to take account of access to the same database record by more than one update or enquiry process. There are two particular concerns:

- entity birth and deletion: the PDI will be called separately for birth of each aspect, but will create only one database record. Similarly, there is only one database record to be deleted

- locking for update and enquiry: the PDI will be called separately for each aspect accessed. It will have to maintain selective locking. When a database record is locked for an event or enquiry, further accesses for the same event or enquiry should be allowed; accesses for other events or enquiries should be locked out.

The PDI must be able to recognise different calls for the same event or enquiry. The system will have to allocate identifiers for event and enquiry instances, which will be passed to the PDI with each call.

7.3 Design optimisation

Single site When applications are to be integrated at a single site, the approach for design optimisation is similar to that for a free-standing application. There are a few additional design options for aspects.

For example, if an aspect has a low rate of activity, it may be moved to a separate table and need not be created until it first becomes active. Suppose that, in Projects-R-Us, only 5% of employees went through training schemes. Rather than having training attributes in every employee row, unused for 95% of instances, we could define a separate employee-training table. The PDI would not create an employee-training row on employee appointment; it would wait until the employee joined their first training scheme.

Chapter 7
Internal Design

As new applications are installed, it would be possible to reduce PDI calls by reading the entire physical record for an entity on the first read and passing aspects' attributes to invoked processes. The reverse would be done for writing back the record. Generally, this is not a good idea:

- it means making changes to already-working applications, beyond the fairly simple 'invoke process for aspect' operations. This increases development and testing requirements

- it reduces physical design options (eg moving aspects to separate tables, as just discussed) and opportunities for reuse of invoked processes (eg in Projects-R-Us, the training component of employee commitments enquiry can be reused to produce the employee personal training schedule).

Distributed systems	Where data is to be distributed there is an additional design issue - minimising the volume of messages passed between sites, since communication between sites is usually both slow and expensive.
	Two design possibilities for overcoming performance problems are data replication and batch messages.
Data replication	Suppose that in Projects-R-Us, the project control and training applications are to be installed at different sites. Personal training schedules for employees are produced in the training application, but need the employee name and department which are maintained in the project control application. If names and departments are duplicated in the training application, no remote access is needed for the production of personal training schedules. Against this, all changes to employee names and departments have to be made at both sites.
Batch messages	In Chapter 6 we argued that when work done on a project is estimated, the project control and time recording processes should be tied together on the two aspects of assignment. If we do not do this, the function has to do a batch update to produce the output.

103

However, we may want to trade simplicity for performance. Suppose that in Projects-R-Us, the project control and time recording applications were to be installed at different sites. If the enquiry process were integrated on the two aspects of assignment, there would have to be a remote call for each instance of assignment.

An alternative is to define separate enquiries in the project control and time-recording systems, each returning a single, batched response. The function would invoke them, and would then have to merge the two sets of results and derive the required output, as described in Chapter 6.

8 Issues

8.1 Introduction

There is limited practical experience of the approach described in this volume. There are some areas in which we need feedback from further practice in order to develop better guidance and heuristics.

8.2 There may be more than one way to partition applications

In Chapter 4 we partitioned the Projects-R-Us overview LDM into two primary applications, project control and training management, and two supporting applications, time recording and the employee server.

However, there are usually other ways in which the LDM could be partitioned. Figure 8.1 shows an alternative for Projects-R-Us.

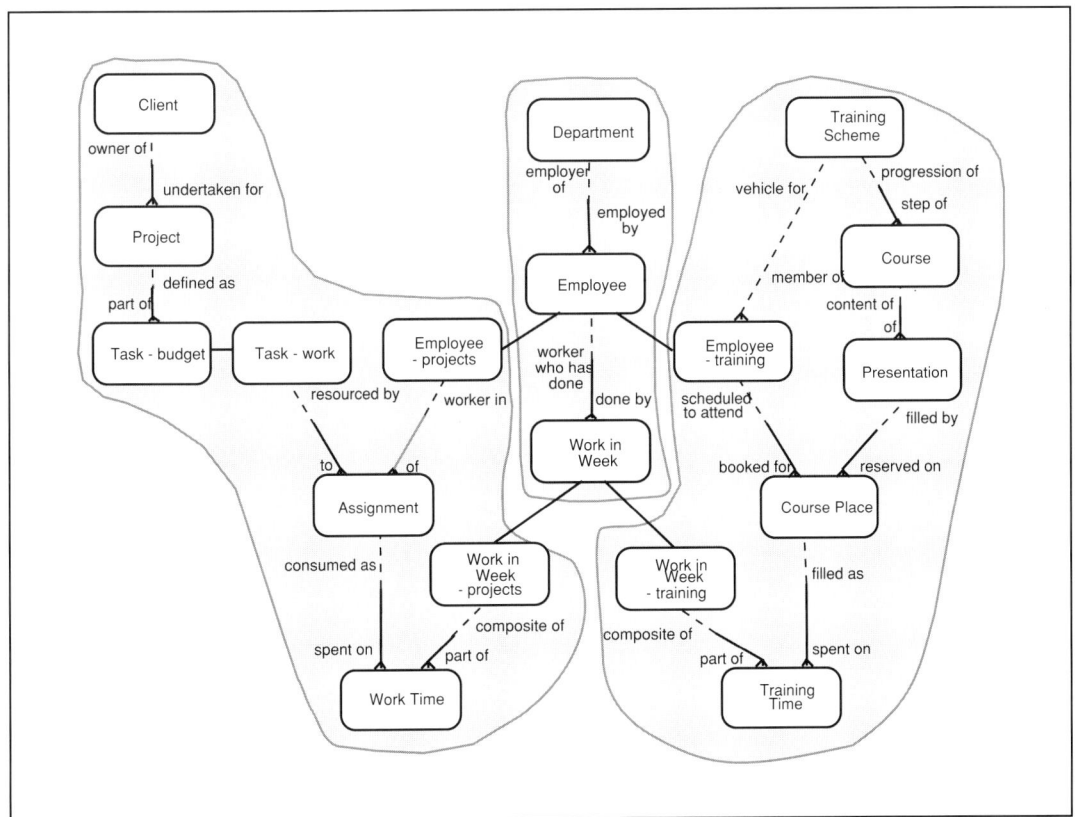

Figure 8.1: Alternative partitioning of the Project-R-Us LDM

There is no 'best' partitioning in any absolute sense. We have to judge what is best in particular circumstances, meeting the users' needs for urgency and priority of delivery of applications while selecting applications that are:

- small and simple enough to be developed significantly faster than a single application for the whole LDM

- large enough that we are delivering significant parts of the functionality with each, and minimising the number of integrations needed

- as self-contained as possible, to minimise the changes needed on integration.

As we use the approach on projects, we should be collecting feedback to reinforce the guidance on partitioning provided in Chapter 4.

8.3 Shared servers may be merged into applications

When several applications share an entity, the simple design approach is to create a shared server. In practice, it is often possible to develop the server as part of a primary application, usually the one that will be implemented first.

There are no hard and fast rules for selecting the order of development but there are two major concerns:

- the sequence in which users want the applications developed

- dependencies between applications. For example, in Projects-R-Us, Assignments (defined in project control) and Course Places (defined in training) have to exist before time can be logged against them.

In Projects-R-Us, we might decide to develop the project control application first, and merge the employee server with the projects aspect of employee. The LDM would be as shown in Figure 8.2.

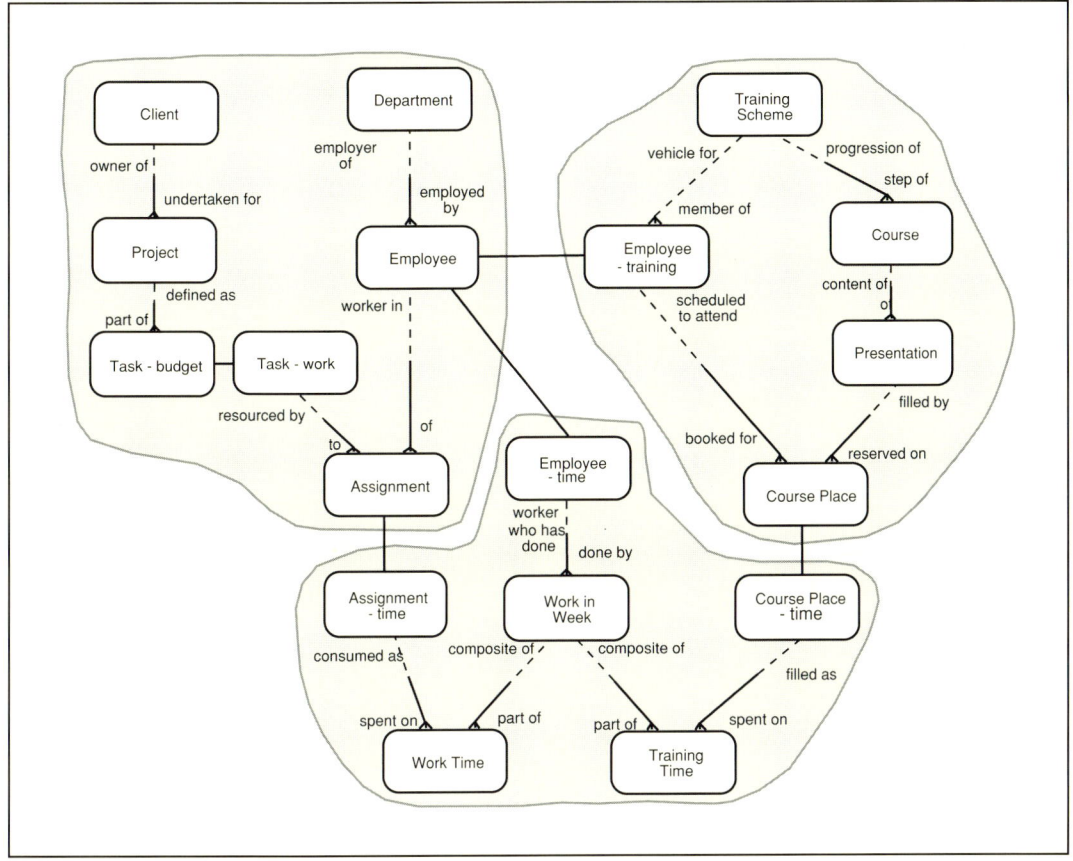

Figure 8.2: Another alternative partitioning of the Project-R-Us LDM

Effect on design approach	Merging a server with an application has no effect on the design principles described in Chapters 4 and 5 - to develop separate Conceptual Models and join them on one-to-one correspondences between aspects.
	It has a minor effect on the detail of the procedure. The application has two roles - to act in its own right, and to be a server for other applications. But the application does not have to act as a server to itself; in the example of Figure 8.2, the Employee and Employee-projects aspects have become the same LDM 'entity'.

Restriction on merging

It may not always be possible to merge aspects; the application aspect may need a separate parallel life in its ELH. For example, in Projects-R-Us, the ELH of Employee-training contains an iterated sequence of joining and leaving Training Schemes, as shown in Figure 8.3.

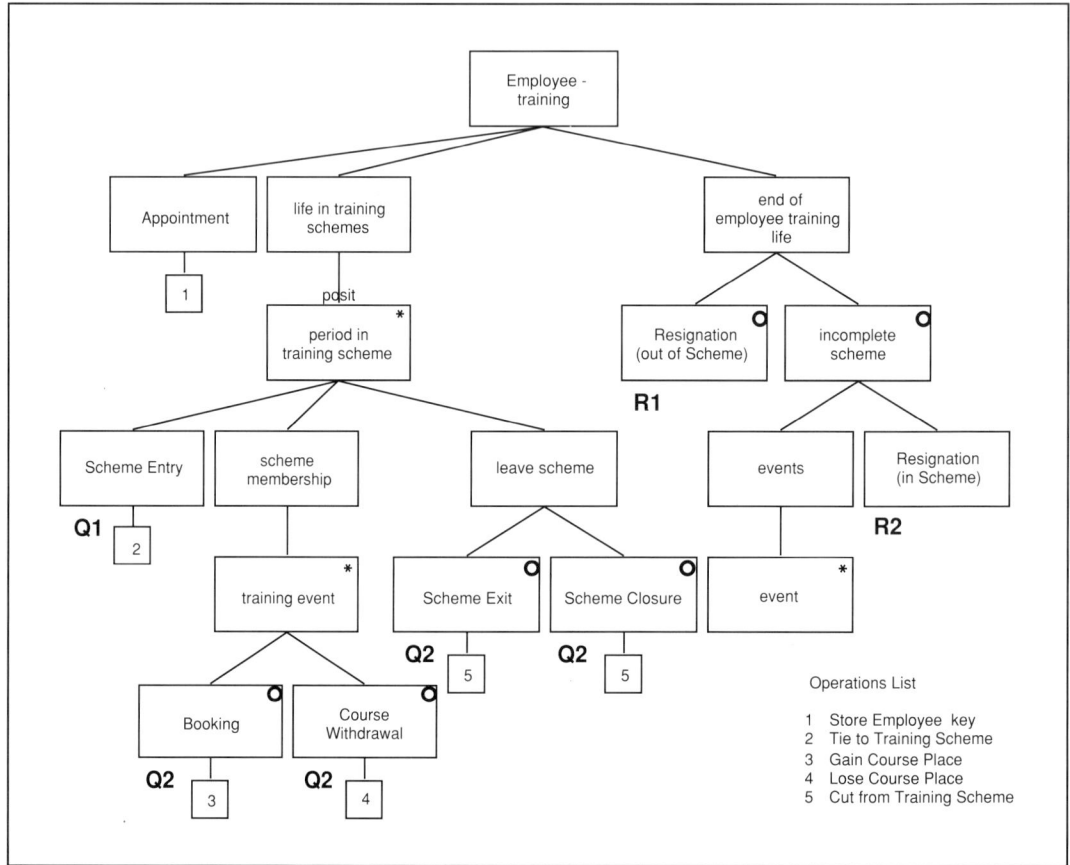

Figure 8.3: Employee-training ELH

The events in the basic aspect of Employee - Name Change, Department Transfer, etc - cannot fit into this ELH; a parallel life is needed. The two aspects have to be modelled separately (although they could be implemented in the same database).

Chapter 8
Issues

8.4 Applications may get out of step

Applications may get out of step during development. The LDM that is partitioned to specify the applications is an overview. The application LDMs will be refined during development. If we have defined applications that are largely self-contained, most LDM changes will be within the scope of individual applications and will not affect integration.

Some changes will affect more than one application. Often, this happens when applications require different views of history in shared data. For example, in Projects-R-Us the employee server started with the simple structure illustrated in Figure 8.4.

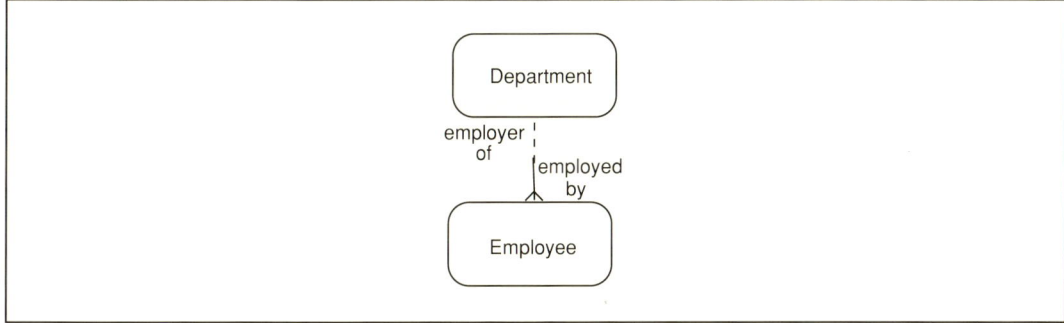

Figure 8.4: Initial LDM for employee server

The project control application needs to enquire on employees in a department when selecting employees for assignment to tasks.

Suppose that during development it became apparent that the training application needed historical data on employees' departments. The employee server would have to support the structure of Figure 8.5.

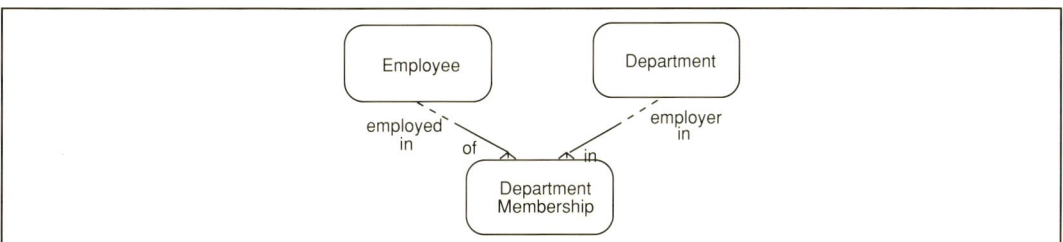

Figure 8.5: Revised LDM for employee server

109

If the project control application and the employee server (as in Figure 8.4) had already been developed and installed, there would be two possibilities:

- restructure the employee server to support the view of Figure 8.5. This would mean replacing the 'employees within department' enquiry for the project control application by an equivalent enquiry on the new structure. Provided that the new enquiry delivered the same results to the External Design, the impact on the project control application would be minimal

- support both current and historical views, as illustrated in Figure 8.6. This would have no impact on the project control application, but would mean a more complex enquiry process to deliver the historical view of department membership to the training application.

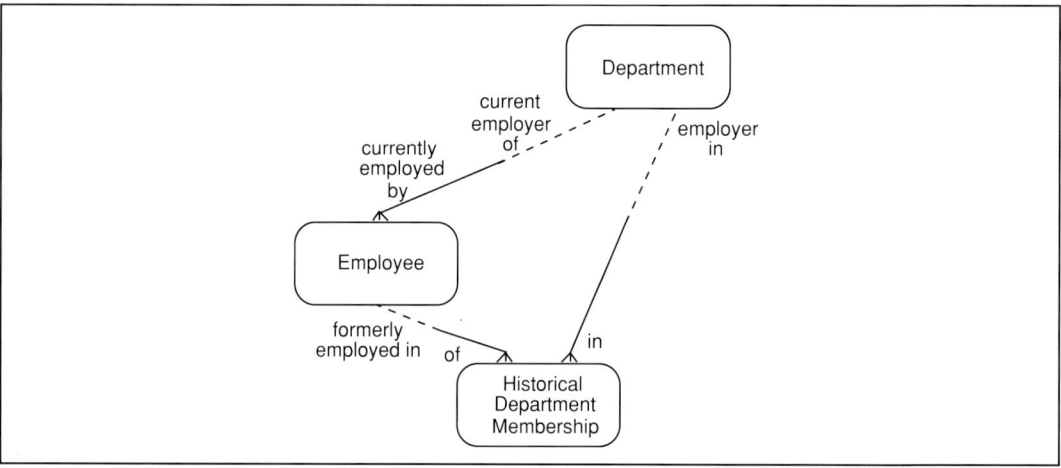

Figure 8.6: Revised LDM for employee server

We need feedback from practice in order to develop heuristics on how to choose between the two approaches in particular situations.

Explicit relationships We could limit restructuring by moving a little away from the relational data model, and using relationship identifiers instead of foreign keys.

For example, suppose we had developed part of the Projects-R-Us time recording application, to support projects. See Figure 8.7.

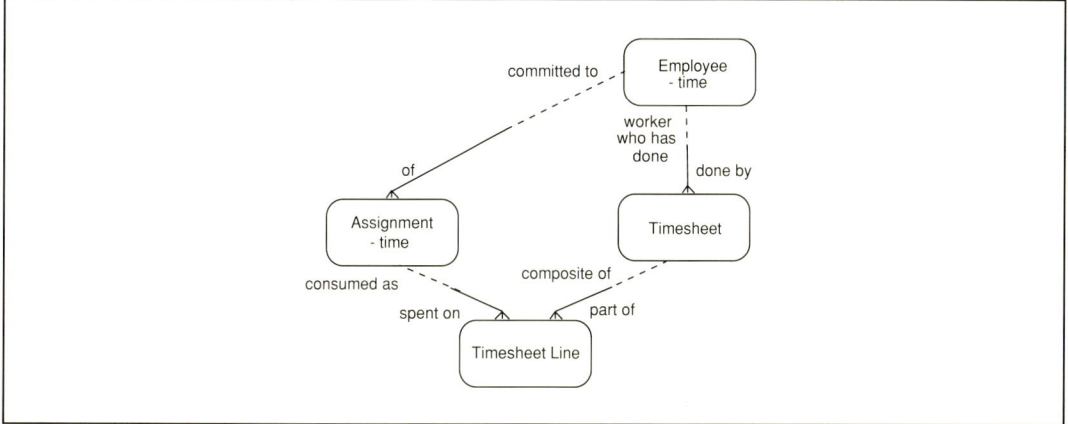

Figure 8.7: Part of the time recording LDM which supporting projects

Then, suppose we want to develop the training management application, so that time recording has to be extended to support training, and to extend time recording further, to accommodate other commitments (holidays, meetings etc). One possibility is as shown in Figure 8.8.

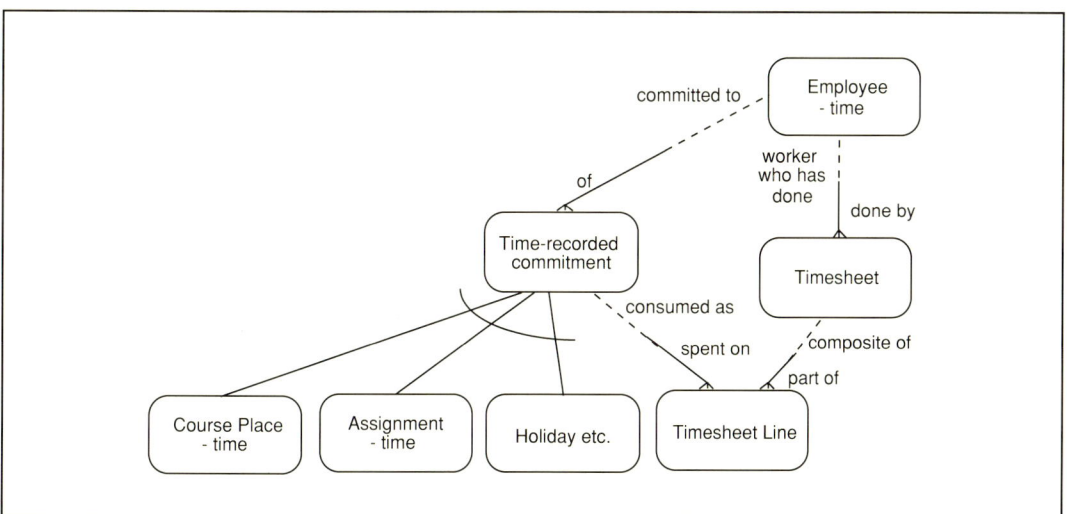

Figure 8.8: Time recording LDM extended to support training and other commitments

The behaviour of timesheet line should not need to change but in the relational model it has a foreign key of assignment identifier, which would have to be replaced by time-recorded-commitment identifier.

What we could do instead is to provide an identifier for each instance of the 'spent on' relationship and use it instead of the assignment identifier in timesheet line. Timesheet line would be owned by 'whatever is on the other end of the "spent on" relationship'.

Operations such as tie, cut and swap in the ELH (carried through into the ECD and UPM), would refer to the relationship, rather than the master entity.

Although this seems like a useful modification, it has some side effects. One is that tools based on the relational model, for example those with SQL or forms-based interfaces, would be more difficult to use. We need some practical experience of this approach.

Partition manager process

Using relationship identifiers instead of foreign keys is one way of supporting the object-oriented concept of encapsulation, which can be viewed in two ways:

- the external view: each object is expected to behave consistently, in terms of its responses to messages sent to it. The rest of the system does not know (or care) what goes on inside the object to produce this behaviour

- the internal view: each object's behaviour can be invoked by other objects in the system. The invoked object has to respond in the expected way to each message sent to it, but does not know (or care) what types of object invoke it.

The Inland Revenue uses encapsulation at the LDM partition level. For implementation, the IR has partitioned its overall LDM into composite objects, similar to the LDM partitions described in this volume (although not necessarily separated on aspects). Each composite object has a manager process which is the buffer between its internal and external behaviours. The manager process provides services in response to requests from other components in the system; updates and enquiries within a composite object are invoked by the manager process.

It will be valuable to obtain feedback on the benefits of this approach as the IR develops further applications.

9 Impact on SSADM Structural Model

9.1 Summary

The approach described in this volume for developing separate applications that are to be integrated is based on five principles:

- applications are defined by identifying distinct areas or types of business activity that require information support, rather than by arbitrary IS or IT decisions

- the content of an application is first defined in its Conceptual Model (LDM, events and enquiries) in the 3-schema Specification Architecture, described in Chapter 2

- an overview LDM is developed and then partitioned to provide LDMs for the applications. Each application LDM is self-contained, with no structural dependencies outside the scope of the application. If an entity type participates in more than one application, an 'aspect' (view) of that entity type is included in the LDM for each relevant application.

This means that we can develop and test each application as a self-contained system, and then 'plug it in' to other applications. (In OO terms, the approach supports encapsulation of each application for processing of persistent data)

- event and enquiry processing is defined within each application. Where an event or enquiry process spans the LDMs of more than one application, there is a simple procedure-call interface (which may be local or remote) between aspects of the same entity (or entities) in different applications

- mapping to a user organisation and an input-output technology (the External Design) and to a data storage and retrieval technology (the Internal Design) are addressed as issues separate from the Conceptual Model.

115

We need only modest extensions of Core SSADM (as defined in the *SSADM V4 Reference Manuals*) to accommodate the approach.

Project structure — There are, broadly, two kinds of project structure; the main difference is the timing of the partitioning of the overall LDM. One uses a preliminary study (which could be an SSADM Feasibility Study or a strategy study) to partition the LDM into substructures to support applications, each of which is then developed as an SSADM project.

The other starts development as a single project and defines subsystems for separate development as part of business system options (SSADM stage 2); each application is then developed as a subproject for stages 3 to 6 of SSADM.

Structural changes — In either case, the required structural changes to SSADM V4 are relatively simple; see Section 9.6.

Products — However, there are three significant changes to the roles of products:

- the need for a specific Business Activity Model; see Section 9.2

- close coupling of the Conceptual Model with the business activity model for specification of applications; see Section 9.3

- reduced emphasis on DFDs as a major 'thread' of development; see Section 9.4.

Techniques — Several SSADM techniques have been modified to address application partitioning and integration. The most significant changes are:

- logical data modelling: extended to support modelling of different aspects (views) of the same entity type in different applications

- function modelling: alternative approaches are suggested for developing DFDs and function definitions when there is no current system, or when the required system will be radically different from the current system

- logical process modelling: development of Effect Correspondence Diagrams and Enquiry Access Paths is extended to include access to logical data (sub)models developed in other applications.

All of the changes are straightforward modifications of the SSADM V4 techniques: see Section 9.5.

Coordination

We shall have to coordinate development of the applications. In the Conceptual Model, applications are integrated in two ways - by sharing data and by handling events and enquiries that cross their boundaries. Application projects will have to work from shared definitions of data (entities, relationships and data items) and events.

In External Design, services from different applications may be invoked from the same user interface; possibly from the same dialogue. Application projects will need a single application style guide and common terminology and names for items displayed in External Design.

Further guidance on coordination of projects is provided in the *Programme and Project Management Library Volumes: An Introduction to Programme Management and A Guide to Programme Management*.

Distributed systems

One reason we might want to integrate separately-developed applications is distribution. Applications that we develop to serve different types of business location may need to share data. If we want a tightly-coordinated system, we shall have to integrate the applications.

This volume deals with partitioning and integration. There is further guidance on distribution in the *ISE Library Volume: Distributed Systems - Application Development*, that complements the approach described in this volume.

9.2 Business Activity Model

One of the foundations of the approach described in this volume is the use of the Conceptual Model of the 3-schema Specification Architecture as the basis of partitioning. We could develop a Conceptual Model without an explicit business activity model (by using the business activities implied by the logical and required data flow models), but it is far easier and more reliable if there is a business activity model. This is especially so when the user organisation and roles may be changed as a result of the SSADM project. The business activity model corresponds to the Business Processing View of Euromethod.

The recommendation is that the business activity model should be one of the working products of the SSADM project, but that the method for developing it should be outside SSADM. The model has to define the business processes to be supported and the information support required.

Approaches

Organisations that already have business modelling methods should be able to use them with SSADM techniques. For organisations that do not have business modelling methods, the Soft Systems Methodology (SSM) is recommended; it is compatible with SSADM and its use is described in the *ISE Library volume: Applying Soft Systems Methodology to an SSADM Feasibility Study*.

Development of the business activity model does not have to affect the structure of SSADM, but it does change the activities within some steps and the products passed between them. The major effects are in steps 120, Investigate and Define Requirements, and 210, Define Business System Options.

User job design — We also have to specify user jobs at the detailed procedural level. This is an important activity whether the developed applications have to be integrated with others or not. Techniques for user job design are outside the scope of SSADM, but complement the SSADM techniques of function definition, dialogue design and batch input-output design.

When applications are to be integrated, it is important to use the same user job design approach and the same application style guide so that users have a 'seamless' view of working practice and the IT support provided by the integrated applications.

9.3 Business Activity Model and Conceptual Model

In the 3-schema Specification Architecture, the Conceptual Model specifies the support for business activity that the required system will provide. It is specified on two levels:

- support for tasks in the business activity model: the outputs needed to support tasks (enquiries), the data needed to support the outputs (LDM) and the updates necessary to maintain the data (events)

- automation of tasks in the business activity model: this does not lead to separate specification components - it extends the scope of events and enquiries. For example, in the projects case study in this volume, when a new task is added to a project, the system has to provide a list of candidate employees from which one will be selected; it could also make the selection automatically.

Applications are defined to support different kinds of business activity. In the case study used in this volume the partitioning into projects, training and time recording was not an arbitrary IS or IT decision - it reflected three different areas of business activity, each with its own objectives, resource requirements, measures of performance and control actions.

This close relationship between business activity and the Conceptual Model should be preserved even when roles and responsibilities change in the organisation; in the External Design, the grouping of events and enquiries into functions will change to conform with changed user roles.

Generally, this separation of Conceptual Model and External Design should be preserved in implementation. If user roles change, the dialogues and batch input-output will have to change but the underlying event and enquiry programs should not need to.

In projects where the organisation is fixed, this separation is not so important. The External Design, represented in DFDs, can be developed in parallel with the Conceptual Model by deriving logical DFDs from current DFDs and extending them into the required DFDs. This is the situation assumed in SSADM V4.

9.4 Current and Required Data Flow Models

In the default structural model of SSADM V4 the functions in the required system are developed in five steps:

- Step 130: the current physical system is described in a data flow model (DFM)

- Step 150: the Current Physical DFM is transformed into a logical DFM of current services

- Step 210: the Current Logical DFM is used as the base for Business System Options. Mandatory new requirements are added and options for non-mandatory new requirements are developed; variants on the IT system boundary are developed

- Step 310: the Required System DFM is formalised from the selected Business System Option

- Step 330: the Required System DFM is decomposed into functions. From this point on the function definitions are the functional specification of the system; the DFDs are used only for presentation.

Chapter 9
Impact on SSADM Structural Model

If current working practice reflects the partitioning of the Conceptual Model - if we can easily draw distinct DFDs of each application, based on current activity - then we can develop the required system DFM as in the SSADM V4 default structural model. If not, we can consider other approaches based on defining functions directly, without deriving them from DFDs.

Functions

In Core SSADM, DFDs have three roles:

- to provide a framework for investigating and documenting current IS activity

- to act as a working definition of IT functionality from which function definitions will be derived

- to provide users with an easily-understood presentation of the required system (and options).

If there is an explicit Business Activity Model, the second of these may change.

Functions support tasks, which are defined as coherent sets of activities in the Business Activity Model, and may be carried out by user roles or by the IT system. Each task requires IT support, consisting of event and enquiry processes in the Conceptual Model.

Functions are of two types, as illustrated in Figure 9.1:

- those that provide IT support for tasks carried out by user roles

- those that provide interfaces between users and automated business tasks.

If we cannot easily develop distinct DFDs of each application from descriptions of current activity, it may be easier to develop functions for each application directly, using the Business Activity Model. For presentation, we can derive the Required System DFDs from the functions.

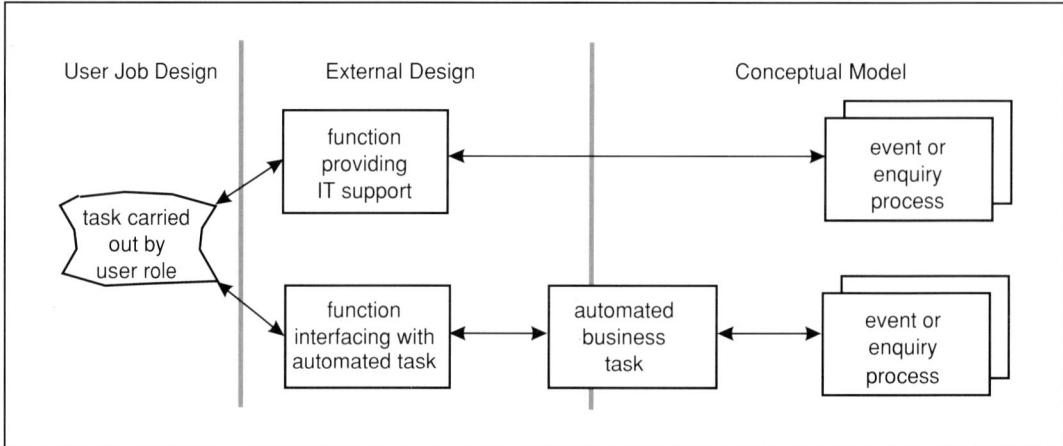

Figure 9.1: The two types of function

No current system

If no current system exists (Core SSADM does not explicitly address this situation), the entity access matrix would support an approach for creating functions and logical DFDs directly:

- events and queries in the entity access matrix can be mapped on to user roles by asking 'Who provides the input?', 'Who uses the output?'

- functions can be built bottom-up by grouping together events and queries for the same user role that serve a common purpose and can be invoked in immediate sequence

- logical DFDs can be built bottom-up by grouping functions for the same user role.

This approach might also be useful if there is a current system but the External Design is likely to be radically different.

Chapter 9
Impact on SSADM Structural Model

9.5 Changes to SSADM V4 Techniques

Data flow modelling

Current DFDs are developed as in Core SSADM, as a means of investigating and documenting current IS activity.

If the existing organisation structure and user roles are not to be changed, required DFDs can be developed as in Core SSADM with one small modification. The consistency check 'every data store must have both input and output data flows somewhere in the DFDs' might fail within a single application. DFDs that describe a single application may update data stores that are used by other applications, and may use data stores that are maintained by other applications.

If the organisation structure and user roles may change, or there is no current system, the approaches described in the previous section may be used instead.

Logical data modelling

Logical data modelling is extended to model entity aspects. If an entity type may participate in more than one application, it is represented in the LDM for each. The result is that each application's LDM is self-contained and the application can be developed and tested independently before integrating it with others.

In most systems there are relatively few entity types that need to be represented in more than one application. In some cases an entity's only responsibility within an application is to exist. Its aspect consists only of its key; other attributes are maintained in another application or a shared server.

Relational data analysis

In RDA, each aspect of an entity can be treated as a separate TNF relation. Ideally, all aspects of the same entity should have the same key. However, some CASE tools automatically consolidate entities with the same key (or do not permit more than one entity definition with the same key). To get round this, it may be necessary to add an attribute to the key, indicating aspect type.

Entity life history analysis	The 'disciplined quit' technique is assumed; this has been accepted by the SSADM Design Authority Board, but is not defined in the *SSADM V4 Reference Manuals*.
	We develop ELHs separately for each application, in Stage 3 of the SSADM project or subproject. This means that if an entity has aspects in several applications we develop an ELH for each.
	There are two modifications of the ELH technique of Core SSADM:
	• identification of events is detached from the remainder of ELH analysis and used in stages 1 and 2. An entity-access matrix is produced, which makes the production of simple ELHs faster and easier in stage 3
	• consistent event names have to be used across applications.
	Two further ELH enhancements are recommended (but are not essential):
	• optimisation of state values (this is described in the *ISE Library Volume: Distributed Systems - Application Development*)
	• use of 'super-events' for identification of reusable processes (described in the *ISE Library Volume: Reuse in SSADM using OO*).
Effect correspondence	Effect correspondences are defined within each application. The technique is extended to deal with communication between applications.
	When an event spans more than one application, the entry point for the entire system is identified within one of them, designated the primary application; it will be invoked by the External Design.
	From the ECD in the primary application, correspondences are indicated with the ECDs in other applications affected

Chapter 9
Impact on SSADM Structural Model

by the event; they will be invoked by the primary application. Each correspondence is one-to-one between different aspects of the same entity.

Invoked applications may themselves invoke further applications.

There is an analogous extension for enquiry access paths.

Logical process models

Update and enquiry process models are derived within each application, as in Core SSADM, with two minor extensions:

- there is an additional operation type 'invoke process, and fail if process fails', which is added to the invoking UPM or EPM wherever there is a correspondence with another application

- some invoked processes for different events may turn out to be identical; they are given a common name. (Note that if 'super-events' are used, many common processes can be identified in development of ELHs).

Function definition

Functions may be developed directly from the business activity model and the Conceptual Model, as described in Section 9.4, rather than being derived from DFDs.

Dialogue design

Dialogues should be developed using a common application style guide. Apart from this, dialogues are developed as in Core SSADM, with one extension, to apply where a dialogue invokes events or enquiries that span more than one application and the applications may not all be delivered at the same time.

When the dialogue is first delivered it may be necessary to include 'stubs' as place markers to remind the user that further services or output are to be delivered later. It may also be necessary to develop stop-gap procedures in user job specifications, to allow users to work around the missing services.

Physical design	The procedure for physical design for integrated applications is very similar to that for freestanding applications, with some additional heuristics.

The most significant change is in the handling of aspects. Several aspects of the same entity may be mapped on to the same table or database file. The recommendation is that this is hidden from the update processes, inside the PDI. |

9.6 SSADM Structural Model

Feasibility Study	One of the options for project structure is to conduct a preliminary study to define the scope of the development and partition the overall LDM into separate applications. The applications can then be developed as a programme of coordinated SSADM projects.

If the preliminary study is conducted as an SSADM Feasibility Study, the Feasibility Module structure of Core SSADM can be used, but some changes are needed to the detail of steps to address:

- development of a business activity model
- partitioning of the overview LDM.

An alternative is to use the approach described in Applying Soft Systems Methodology to an SSADM Feasibility Study, which produces a Soft Systems model of business activities. |
| Step 010: Prepare for Feasibility Study | The Project Initiation Document should provide an initial view of user requirements/expectations for separate applications and the sequence in which they must be delivered. |
| Step 020: Define the Problem | In addition to the activities in Core SSADM, a business activity model should be produced. It should describe what the business has to do rather than how it is done |

and who does it. Areas of business activity that are candidates for support by separately-developed applications should be identified.

A single overview LDM should be developed, covering the scope of the whole business area to be supported.

Step 030: Select Feasibility Options	Feasibility study options must address the possibilities for partitioning the logical data model into different applications.

Generally, one partitioning will be selected as the required option, but a possible outcome is that partitioning is not necessary - one application will be developed. |
| **Step 040: Assemble Feasibility Report** | The Feasibility Report must address application partitioning and integration requirements in addition to the contents defined in the *SSADM V4 Reference Manuals*. It must specify a separate project for each partition of the LDM in the selected option, and the approach for coordination of the projects, conforming for example with the guidance in the *PPM Library Volume: A Guide to Programme Management*. |
| **Projects in a programme: stages 1 and 2** | For separate projects specified in a preliminary study, stages 1 and 2 of SSADM are very similar to Core SSADM. The differences are:

- the business activity model may partially supplant the role of the DFM, as described in Sections 9.2 to 9.4

- an entity access matrix is developed in step 150, Derive Logical View of Current Services, to confirm the scope of the LDM for support of business activity

- development of Business System Options is constrained by the requirement to fit in with the other projects in the programme. |

From stage 3 on, the project structure is very similar to that for subprojects, described next.

Subprojects starting from a single project: Stages 1 and 2

If the scope is well-defined and it is known that separate applications will be needed - for example, when parallel work is needed to meet delivery timescales, or when a tightly-coordinated distributed system is required - a single project may be undertaken for stages 1 and 2 and then partitioned into separate subprojects for stages 3 to 6.

Stage 1: Investigation of Current Environment

No structural change of stage 1 is needed. Some changes are needed to the detail of steps.

Step 110: Establish Analysis Framework

As for the Feasibility Study, the Project Initiation Document should provide an initial view of user requirements/ expectations for separate applications and the sequence in which they must be delivered.

Planned project activities, end-product definitions and plans for involvement of users must all take account of integration issues.

Step 120: Investigate and Define Requirements

A business activity model is developed, and the requirements are defined in terms of information support needed by the business activity model. The business activity model may partially supplant the role of the DFM, as described in Sections 9.2 to 9.4.

Step 130: Investigate Current Processing

The procedure is unchanged.

Step 140: Investigate Current Data

Unchanged. The LDM is developed as a single model for the entire system (not as separate LDMs for each application).

Chapter 9
Impact on SSADM Structural Model

Step 150: Derive Logical View of Current Services

The procedure includes an additional technique, event identification, and some of the guidelines for development of the DFM and LDM are different:

Data Flow Model

If the organisation structure and user roles are fixed, the logical DFM is derived from the current physical DFM. It is built from the bottom up, around user roles (this is one of three possibilities recommended in the *SSADM V4 Reference Manuals*).

If user roles are to change significantly, a different approach might be used: functions may be defined by grouping events and enquiries that serve the same user role. The logical DFM can be built bottom-up from functions, and reconciled with the current physical DFM to ensure that no essential current processes have been omitted.

Logical Data Model

The procedure for validating the LDM is extended a little. As each process is used to validate the LDM:

- a list of attributes is built up for each entity type (ask 'What attributes are needed in this entity to support this process?')
- enquiry rows in the entity access matrix are created.

Entity Access Matrix

The entity access matrix is an extension of the idea of the entity-event matrix; it includes access to entities for enquiries as well as updates.

Once the attributes and relationships in the LDM are known, the LDM can be analysed to determine the events essential to keeping the database up-to-date. Enquiries will have already been included in the matrix during validation of the LDM.

Step 160: Assemble Investigation Results	The procedure is unchanged.
Stage 2: Business System Options	In order to deal with partitioning and, possibly, distribution issues, Business System Options have to be developed in greater detail than in Core SSADM V4.

If a distributed system is to be developed, business system options are developed in two parts, functional options and distribution options. See the *ISE Library Volume: Distributed Systems - Application Development* for further information.

Otherwise, the structure of stage 2 is retained, but the procedure within step 210 is more elaborate. |
| Step 210: Define Business System Options | In addition to the concerns of Core SSADM - how current problems will be resolved, which functional requirements that are not supported in current system will be met, what the impact on users will be - options for partitioning also have to be considered.

The emphasis for developing options will vary from project to project:

- the range of options for new functionality may be wide, with limited possibilities for partitioning

- there may be several options for partitioning, with limited requirements for new functionality.

Where there are wide-ranging options for both functionality and partitioning, it may be better to develop options in two passes - first agree the required functionality, then the partitioning.

The Entity Access Matrix, developed in step 150, is used both to identify partitioning options and to identify events and enquiries that span partitions (and hence the required communication between applications). |

Chapter 9
Impact on SSADM Structural Model

The LDM must be elaborated to support additional requirements not provided by current IT systems. The procedure is:

- define the outputs needed to support each new functional requirement in the selected business option; validate the LDM to ensure that they can be delivered; define LDM attributes

- analyse the LDM's attributes and relationships to identify events; extend the entity access matrix

- identify the user role that supplies the input and receives the output for each type of event

- add volumes to the entity access matrix.

This means that the LDM is substantially more developed in stage 2 than if Core SSADM were used.

Step 220: Select Business System Option

The general approach in this step is not changed.

Coordination of projects in Stages 3 to 6

Whether applications are being developed as separate projects in a programme, or subprojects of a single development, the approach for SSADM stages 3 to 6 is similar. Development of each application is managed as for stand-alone SSADM projects, with the addition of the following configuration management activities:

- maintenance of a common dictionary of event names

- maintenance of a common dictionary of entity and attribute names, at least for shared entities (ie those that have been split into aspects); when new attributes are needed for an aspect within an application, they should be identified as application-specific, or shared (in which case they should be added to a 'shared server' aspect)

- provision of a common application style guide

131

- provision of a common technical architecture, if possible; if not, ensuring that different technical architectures for applications can support the required communication

- ensuring that interfaces between applications are consistent from both the invoking and invoked processes' views.

Stage 3: Requirements Specification	There is no need for structural change to Requirements Specification. The main change is that some of the work done in this stage in Core SSADM has already been done in stage 2.
Step 310: Define Required System Processing	No change is needed to the procedure in this step; production of the required DFDs is slightly simplified:

- level-2 DFDs have been partly developed in the creation of Business System Options

- DFDs are already organised by user role

- new functional requirements have been mapped to events and enquiries - their scope, input and output should be fairly well-understood.

Step 320: Develop Required Data Model	Much of the work described for this step in the *SSADM V4 Reference Manual* has been done in Business System Options.
Step 330: Derive System Functions	Identification of functions is simplified - DFDs are organised as groups of functions serving user roles.
	There is a stronger correspondence between functions and events/enquiries than in Core SSADM. Events and enquiries are identified as supporting user tasks in the business activity model. Functions provide the 'packaging' of events and enquiries to support user roles for carrying out the corresponding user tasks, for the External Design.

Chapter 9
Impact on SSADM Structural Model

Step 340: Enhance Required Data Model	No change is needed to the procedure in this step, although there are minor changes to the Relational Data Analysis technique, concerned with keys and entity aspects.
Step 350: Develop Specification Prototypes	The technique is as for Core SSADM, with one significant extension.
	Where a prototype demonstrates a dialogue that spans multiple applications, and the applications are to be delivered at different times, the prototype should make the user aware of the functionality that will be supported as each application is delivered.
	This will be an important source of requirements for short-term measures while the user is waiting for later applications.
Step 360: Develop Processing Specification	The differences from Core SSADM V4 are:

- simple Entity Life Histories are easier to develop, since the entity access matrix has been produced in stage 2

- there are two changes to the ELH analysis technique to deal with entity aspects and disciplined quits; two further ELH changes, for optimisation of entity states and the use of 'super-events' for reusable processes, are recommended but not mandatory

- development of Effect Correspondence Diagrams and Enquiry Access Paths has to take account of events and enquiries that span more than one application.

These changes may mean that in a few cases it is not possible to identify correspondences that link all effects into a single network, with a different entry point for each fragment.

Step 370: Confirm System Objectives	The procedure is unchanged.
Step 380: Assemble Requirements Specification	The procedure is unchanged.

Stage 4: Technical System Options

Step 410: Define Technical Options	The procedure is generally the same as in the *SSADM V4 Reference Manuals,* but there may be a well-defined technical architecture with which all the applications have to conform.
	If not, later-delivered applications have to take account of the technology used for earlier applications, and ensure that the technical options all support communication between applications.
Step 420: Select Technical System Options	The procedure is unchanged.

Stage 5: Logical Design — No structural change is needed for this stage.

Step 510: Design User Dialogues	Generally unchanged. However, if a dialogue invokes processes that span multiple applications, and they will not all be delivered when the dialogue is first delivered, the screen formats may have to include place markers for data dependent on the missing applications.
	There should be a consistent application style guide for all the applications in a programme.

Chapter 9
Impact on SSADM Structural Model

Step 520: Define Update Processing

The procedure is unchanged, but the technique for defining update processing is extended to cover:

- invocation of an event process in one application by a process for the same event in another application

- where there are multiple correspondences between invoked and invoking ECDs, breaking down the ECD for the invoked process into several partial processes to avoid ambiguous references to entities ('LDM loops')

- identification of common invoked processes.

There is additional guidance for distributed systems, including possibilities for OO and client/server specifications, in the *ISE Library Volume: Distributed Systems: Application Development*.

Step 530: Define Enquiry Processing

The same options exist for enquiry processes as for update processes.

Step 540: Assemble Logical Design

The procedure is unchanged.

Stage 6: Physical Design

The scope of this guide does not extend to the detail of physical design, but an overview of the approach is useful.

Physical design in SSADM V4 is more general than stages 1 to 5. It provides guidance on how to specify the physical design method, rather than being the specific physical design method.

Feedback from projects using the approach in this guide with a range of technology will be essential for the development of more detailed guidance for physical design.

Step 610: Prepare for Physical Design	The procedure is similar to that in the *SSADM V4 Reference Manuals*. The classification system for database storage and performance may need to be extended:

- if application databases are to be implemented on different DBMSs, the classification schemes need to include the mechanisms for calls between DBMSs (eg gateways, heterogeneous client/server)

- if application databases are to be implemented at different locations, the classification schemes need to include the mechanisms for calls across the network (eg remote database access, client/server).

In this step, timing forms (or spreadsheets) are developed for the selected DBMS. Timing forms for transactions that span multiple locations or DBMSs should include communication between the databases and across the network, where appropriate. |
| Step 620: Create Physical Data Design | The procedure for First-cut Data Design is generally as described in the *SSADM V4 Reference Manuals*; the first-cut rules differ slightly to take account of multiple aspects of the same entity types:

- if aspects of an entity are to be implemented on the same DBMS at the same location, define them as views of the same underlying table or database file

- otherwise, define aspects as distinct database tables or record types. Ensure that aspects of the same entity have a common external identifier (such as Client Number) that can be used to select an entity instance consistently across all its aspects. |
| Step 630: Create Function Component Implementation Map | Creation of the Function Component Implementation Map should be in one way slightly easier than in Core SSADM. The separation of concerns imposed by the 3-schema Specification Architecture means that common components at the level of event, enquiry, I/O structure and format should be clearly visible. |

Chapter 9
Impact on SSADM Structural Model

The possibility that some database processes may be partitioned across several DBMSs makes it more difficult to provide general guidance on creating the FCIM, especially on the use of common components, although it is often clear what is needed in specific situations. More feedback from practice is needed.

Step 640: Optimise Physical Data Design

The general idea of physical design optimisation is as in the *SSADM V4 Reference Manuals*. If databases are to be implemented on different DBMSs and/or at different locations, additional performance trade-offs may be possible by:

- replicating data

- batching communication between physical databases where, in the first cut design, there are multiple correspondences (multiple entity types and/or multiple instances of the same entity type).

Step 650: Complete Function Specification

There is only one significant difference from the *SSADM V4 Reference Manuals*. The function, as represented in the External Design, needs to invoke Conceptual Model processes (implemented as database update and enquiry programs), which may span several applications.

If applications are to be delivered at different times, data delivered to the user from functions (via dialogues or batch I/O) may have to include 'stubs' or place markers for data from applications that will be delivered later than the first provision of the function.

Step 660: Consolidate Process Data Interface

There are some additional requirements of the PDI in a coordinated system of separately-developed applications:

- where aspects of the same entity are mapped on to a single physical table or record type, the PDI may have to take account of access to the same database record by more than one update or enquiry process

137

- where a record instance may be hit by more than one message for the same event, the PDI may have to manage selective locking, so that other events and enquiries are locked out but multiple messages for the same event are allowed in. The system will have to allocate identifiers for event and enquiry instances, which will be passed to the PDI with each call.

Step 670: Assemble Physical Design	The procedure is unchanged.

Bibliography

CCTA Information Systems Engineering (ISE) Library

SSADM and Client/Server Applications,
HMSO, 1994, ISBN 0 11 330624 5

Distributed Systems: Application Development,
HMSO, 1994, ISBN 0 11 330623 7

Reuse in SSADM using OO,
HMSO, 1994, ISBN 0 11 330621 0

An Introduction to Reuse,
HMSO, 1994, ISBN 0 11 330625 3

Managing Reuse,
HMSO, 1994, ISBN 0 11 330616 4

Applying Soft Systems Methodology to an SSADM Feasibility Study,
HMSO, 1993, ISBN 0 11 330601 6

Database Language SQL Explained,
HMSO, 1993, ISBN 0 11 330583 4

CASE and the Issues for IS Management,
HMSO, 1994, ISBN 0 11 330594 X

CCTA Information Management (IM) Library

Corporate Data Modelling,
HMSO, 1994, ISBN 0 11 330614 8

Data Management,
HMSO, 1994, ISBN 0 11 330634 2

CCTA Programme & Project Management (PPM) Library

An Introduction to Programme Management,
HMSO, 1994, ISBN 0 11 330611 3

A Guide to Programme Management,
HMSO, 1994, ISBN 0 11 330600 8

Volumes in the ISE, IM and PPM Libraries are available by mail, fax and telephone orders from:

HMSO Publications Centre
PO Box 276
London
SW8 5DT

Telephone orders from outside UK +44-171-873-9090
(from within UK 0171-873-9090)
General enquiries from outside UK +44-171-873-0011
(from within UK 0171-873-0011)
(queuing system in operation for both numbers)

Alternatively, they may be purchased from HMSO Bookshops, HMSO's Accredited Agents and through good booksellers.

Euromethod

Euromethod
CCTA IS Notice 71, 1994

For a copy please contact the CCTA Library on tel: 01603 703350.

Euromethod Delivery Planning Guide, Deliverable 2.3, EM-2.3-DPG, 1994, Euromethod Project

Euromethod Concepts Manual 2 Deliverable Model, Deliverable 3.2, EM-3.2-DM, 1994, Euromethod Project

SSADM

The SSADM V4 Reference Manuals (ISBN 1 85554 004 5) are published in the UK by NCC Blackwell Ltd and are available from The Publications Manager, National Computer Centre Ltd, Oxford Road, Manchester M1 7ED.

Information packs on SSADM are available from the International SSADM Users Group (ISUG):
tel: +44-1959-534337 (01959 534337 from within UK) and fax: +44-1959-534184 (01959 534184 from within UK).

'Quits and Resumes on Entity Life Histories: A Comparison of Alternative Approaches', ISUG Technical Committee, 1993, This paper is available from ISUG on the same numbers as above.

Glossary

3-schema Specification Architecture
A framework for IT system specification and implementation in which the IS services needed to support business activities are defined in a Conceptual Model. The mappings from the Conceptual Model to specific user organisations and implementation technologies are defined in an External Design and an Internal Design. In SSADM V4 the concepts of the 3-schema Specification Architecture are embodied in the Universal Function Model.

aggregation
An object-oriented term describing classes which are composed of (or consist of) other classes.

aspect
An application's view of a real-world entity type, which models part of the behaviour of the entity type. What is usually called 'an entity' on an LDM is really an aspect, since it represents only a partial view of the world entity type. In most cases a real-world entity type has only one LDM aspect; there is no confusion in referring to 'LDM entities'. Aspects have to be distinguished only when there are multiple views of the same entity type that have to be coordinated in some way.

asynchronous cycles
Behaviour of an entity type that cannot be modelled in a simple ELH - there is at least one constrained sequence or cycle of events in the real-world behaviour that cannot be modelled as successive states, because unrelated events can occur at unpredictable points. The SSADM V4 solution is to include parallel lives in the ELHs. The recommendation in this guide is to model the asynchronous cycles of behaviour in separate aspects.

attribute
A descriptive property of an object class or entity that can take different values. The values of the attribute vary both with the instance of the object class or entity under consideration and with the time at which the instance is considered.

Business Process Model
A model of real-world business activities.

Business Process View (BPV)	A Euromethod term describing a model of real-world business activities.
CASE	Computer Assisted Software Engineering.
class	An object-oriented term for a set of object instances of the same type. A class defines the methods and the attributes of the object instances.
class hierarchy	An object-oriented term for a hierarchy of classes in which subtypes inherit the methods and attributes of their supertypes.
class instance	See object.
Conceptual Model	The Conceptual Schema in the 3-schema Specification Architecture, called a *model* to emphasise that it is a partial model of the business, developed by a process of analysis and discovery. It specifies the required IT services as: information support needed by business activities; data needed to provide it; processes needed to keep the data up-to-date. It also defines which business activities are to be automated. It described the services independently of the user organisation structure and the technology for implementation. In SSADM the Conceptual Model consists of the LDM, ECDs/UPMs and EAPs/EPMs, and the implemented update and enquiry processes.
Conceptual Schema	See Conceptual Model.
Core SSADM	The five SSADM V4 modules as described in the *SSADM V4 Reference Manuals*.
correspondence	In an ECD, the indication that effects on two different entities are in one-to-one correspondence, shown by joining them with an arrow. ECD correspondences are permitted only between entities (or aspects) connected directly by relationships in the LDM.
Data Flow Diagram	Shows how services are organised and processing is undertaken. It should be a simple diagram that is readily understood, so that it can act as an effective means of communication between analysts and users.

Glossary

Data Flow Model A set of Data Flow Diagrams and their associated documentation. The diagrams form a hierarchy with the Data Flow Diagram Level 1 showing the scope of the system and the lower level diagrams expanding the detail as appropriate. Additional documentation provides a description of the processes, input/output data flows and external entities.

DBMS Acronym for Database Management System.

DFD See Data Flow Diagram.

DFM See Data Flow Model.

Disciplined Quit A technique for modelling recognition problems in ELHs. It is more formal than the alternative, the undisciplined quit, and provides better support for automating the derivation of ECDs and UPMs from ELHs. The major differences from the undisciplined quit are: the scope of the recognition problem must be defined by *posit* and *admit* labels; *Quit/Resume* means 'the event labelled with R(*esume*) may occur <u>instead of</u> the event labelled with Q(*uit*)'.

EAP See Enquiry Access Path.

ECD See Effect Correspondence Diagram.

Effect Correspondence Diagram Shows all the effects an event has on data within the system and how those effects impact upon each other.

Effect Correspondence Diagrams provide the access path details for update functions which are used in logical design activities.

ELH See Entity Life History.

encapsulation An object-oriented term describing the property of objects whereby the methods of any object cannot access the attributes of any other object.

Enquiry Access Path The route through the Logical Data Model from an entry point to the entity, or entities, required for a particular enquiry function.

143

Enquiry Process Model	Consists of a structure diagram for an enquiry processing requirement and the associated Operations List. The structure is based on the Enquiry Access Path.
Entity Life History	Charts all of the events that may cause a particular entity to be changed in any way. It shows the valid structure of events (initially identified through the use of data flow modelling and function definition techniques) affecting an entity on the Logical Data Structure.
EPM	See Enquiry Process Model.
Euromethod	A major European Union initiative to provide a public domain 'framework' for the planning, procurement and management of services for the investigation, development or amendment of information systems.
event	An event is identified as whatever triggers a process (on a Data Flow Diagram) to update the values or status of the system. An event may cause more than one entity to be changed. In the logical system, an event initiates an update process.
External Design	The External Schema in the 3-schema Specification Architecture, called a design to emphasise that it is developed by a process of design and engineering - there is no 'right' answer. It is defined as a two-level mapping. Update and enquiry processes in the Conceptual Model are mapped on to functions that support user roles in a particular user organisation. Functions are grouped into dialogues and/or batch input-output programs that are then mapped to an input-output technology.
External Schema	See External Design.
function	A set of system processing which the users wish to schedule together, to support their business activity.
inheritance	An object-oriented term describing the property of classes which allows subtypes in a hierarchy of class types to automatically take on the methods and

Glossary

	attributes of all their supertypes, before adding methods and attributes of their own.
incremental delivery	An approach to development in which: releases of the implemented system are delivered within relatively short intervals; each release extends the scope of the system and is integrated with the functionality of previous releases.
instance variable	See attribute.
Internal Design	The Internal Schema in the 3-schema Specification Architecture, called a design to emphasise that it is developed by a process of design and engineering - there is no 'right' answer. The LDM in the Conceptual Model is mapped on to a data storage and access technology to produce a database design. Stored data is presented to implemented update and enquiry processes by a PDI, as if it were stored in the LDM.
Internal Schema	See Internal Design.
IR	Inland Revenue.
LDM	See Logical Data Model.
LDM partition	Substructure of an LDM that supports an application system or subsystem to be developed (almost) independently and then integrated with applications based on other partitions of the same LDM. Partitions are created by splitting shared entities into aspects, so that each partition is a self-contained LDM, linked to other partitions by one-to-one correspondences. This partitioning provides robustness in design - each application could be implemented as a free-standing system (although perhaps with some gaps in its output until data from other applications is available) - and simple linkage of related processes in different applications.
Logical Data Model	Provides an accurate model of the information requirements of all or part of an organisation. This serves as a basis for file and database design, but is

independent of any specific implementation technique or product.

The Logical Data Model consists of a Logical Data Structure, Entity Descriptions and Relationship Descriptions. Associated descriptions of attribute/data items and grouped domains are maintained in the Data Catalogue.

message passing An object-oriented term describing the way in which objects communicate with each other.

method (object-oriented) An object-oriented term implying the part of an object permitted to read and update specific object attributes.

object An instance of an object class comprising both the methods of the object class and attributes with particular values.

object attribute See attribute.

object class See class.

operations list A list of all the operations on either an Enquiry Process Model or an Update Process Model.

parallel lives The approach in SSADM V4 for modelling asynchronous cycles in a single ELH, suitable for modelling within an application. This guide recommends using distinct aspects with separate ELHs, for three reasons: aspects address more general concepts of parallel behaviour, of which the parallel ELH within an application is a special case; aspects provide possibilities for partitioning within an application, to allow analysis and logical design to proceed in parallel; there are some situations that cannot be modelled with parallel lives.

PDI See Process-data Interface.

process-data interface Documents how the Logical Data Model can be mapped onto the Physical Data Design, showing how it interfaces with the Physical Processing Specification. The PDI allows the designer to implement the logical update and enquiry processes as physical programs, independently of the physical database structure.

relation A logical file of records in a relational database. A relation must have a unique key; the order of the rows and columns is not significant; each column must have a unique name; no duplicate rows are allowed. A relation is more commonly referred to as a 'table'.

recognition problem A situation sometimes encountered in development of ELHs in which an event could start either of two different sequences, but when the event occurs it is impossible to recognise what the final outcome will be. The solution is to make an assumption and proceed until some subsequent event either confirms it or proves it wrong. If it is proven wrong the entity's state needs to be changed to reflect the recognised situation, and any unwanted side effects of the incorrect assumption (eg changes to attributes) have to be reversed. This may be modelled by either a disciplined quit or an undisciplined quit. Recognition problems may occur in models of other types of serial structure, including UPMs, EPMs, dialogue navigation structures and Jackson program structures.

Requirements Analysis The objective is to produce the Analysis of Requirements. Within this the Selected Business System Option will define the scope of further investigation. This Module has two Stages:

- Stage 1 Investigation of Current Environment
- Stage 2 Business System Options.

Requirements Catalogue The central repository for information covering all identified requirements, both functional and non-functional. Each entry is textual and describes a required facility or feature of the proposed system.

SSADM Rationale A definition of the essential characteristics of SSADM, described in the *ISE Library volume: Customising SSADM*

Soft Systems Methodology A methodology directed at modelling of Human Activity Systems [see *Systems Thinking, Systems Practice by*

Checkland P.B. and published in 1981 by John Wiley and Sons], which may be mapped on to organisation structures to describe business systems, and which often need support from IT systems. CCTA's *ISE Library Volume: Applying Soft Systems Methodology to an SSADM Feasibility Study* describes how Soft Systems Methodology can be used in an SSADM Feasibility Study.

SSM	See Soft Systems Methodology
super-event	A common process identified as a selection component in an ELH, invoked by each of the events in the selection. The super-event may be propagated through other ELHs instead of the events that select it; this leads to simpler ELHs and a common UPM. Super-events are described more fully in the *ISE Library Volume: Reuse in SSADM using OO*.
TNF	An abbreviation for third normal form. It describes the state of data after the application of the first three relational data analysis techniques.
TNF relation	A relation that is in third normal form. Relations may exist in fourth or higher normal forms.
undisciplined quit	A technique for modelling recognition problems in ELHs. It is less formal than the alternative, the disciplined quit. The major differences from the undisciplined quit are: *Quit/Resume* means 'the event labelled with R(*esume*) may occur <u>after</u> the event labelled with Q(*uit*)'; the scope of the recognition problem is not defined (*Quits* and *Resumes* may be placed wherever they are needed). The approach can provide good descriptions of recognition problems and their solutions but not formal specifications, because Quits and Resumes can over-ride the structure of the ELH. This means that some ELHs cannot be validated automatically and possibilities for automated derivation of ECDs and UPMs are limited.
Update Process Model	Is a structure diagram for update (event) processing and the associated operations list. The UPM is based on the Entity Life Histories, which provide a data-oriented view of the system, and the associated Effect Correspondence

Glossary

Diagrams, which provide an event-oriented or process-oriented view of the system.

UPM See Update Process Model.

user role A user role is defined as a collection of job holders who share a large proportion of common tasks for which they may need support from an IT system.

Index

3-schema Specification Architecture 7, 9, 10, 21, 27, 29, 30, 90, 115, 118, 119, 136, 141, 142, 144, 145
   3 schemata are implemented as code 11, 30
   conceptual model 9-14, 28, 29, 43, 45, 87, 89, 90, 94, 97, 98, 115-121, 125, 137, 141, 142, 144, 145
   conceptual schema 24, 26-28, 142
   discovery versus design 28
   external design 10, 11, 13, 14, 29, 57, 89-91, 93-98, 110, 115, 117, 120, 122, 124, 132, 137, 141, 144
   external schema 27, 28, 144
   internal design 10, 11, 13, 15, 29, 37, 101, 115, 141, 145
   internal schema 27, 29, 145
   three schemata 10, 11, 21
   See also: Conceptual Model, Conceptual Schema, External Design, External Schema, Internal Design and Internal Schema.
Application 7-13, 31, 32, 34, 37, 38, 40, 43-45, 47, 49, 51-54, 56, 57, 59, 63, 64, 78-80, 82-85, 84-86, 89, 91-95, 97, 99, 101-103, 106-111, 115, 115-119, 121, 123-125, 128, 130, 131, 133-136, 139, 141, 145, 146, 148
   application partitioning 9, 11, 14, 21, 116, 127
   See also: Partitioning and Conceptual Model.
Aspect 11-13, 31-33, 35-38, 40, 49, 50, 56, 57, 59-63, 87, 101-103, 106, 108, 115, 123, 131, 141
   aspects and aggregation 40
   aspects and inheritance 39
   aspects and subtypes 40
   aspects identified in analysis of parallel life histories 62
   base aspect 36, 59
   basic existence 36, 38, 49
   coordination of behaviour 12, 32
   corporate aspect 36
   LDM representation 32
   restrictions on merging 108
   using aspects to decompose and isolate areas of a data model 47
   what is an aspect? 38
Basis of approach 12

Batch 11, 119, 120, 137, 144
  batched response 104
  batch input-output 27, 29, 89, 119, 120, 144
  batch process 94
  batch update 95, 103
Business 10, 11, 13, 15, 21-28, 31, 33, 40, 43-45, 47, 52, 89, 94, 115-121, 125-128, 130-132, 141, 142, 144, 147, 148
  Business activities 23-26, 52, 89, 118, 126, 141, 142, 144
  Business activity 11, 15, 44, 45, 89, 94, 115, 116, 118, 119, 121, 125-128, 132
Business process model 141
Business Process View
  See: Euromethod.
Business System Options 120, 131, 147
Changes to SSADM V4 techniques 123
Client/server 14, 87, 135, 136, 139
Communication
  between applications 14
  DFD as effective means of 142
  ECD extensions to cope with communication between locations 124
  failure of communications between locations 36
  identifying communication requirements between locations 130
  overcoming performance problems 103
  physical design optimisation 87, 103, 137
  support for from different technical architectures 132, 134
  timing forms 136
  with server 34
Conceptual model 9-14, 28, 29, 43, 45, 87, 89, 90, 94, 97, 98, 115-121, 125, 137, 141, 142, 144, 145
  See also: Conceptual schema.
  integrating separately-developed conceptual models 10, 14
  joining on one-to-one correspondences 107
  See also: Integrating.
  partitioning the conceptual model 9, 14, 43, 89, 90
  See also: Partitioning and Application.
  simulation of the business 21
Conceptual schema 24, 26-28, 142
  See also: Conceptual Model.
Configuration management 131-132
Coordinated system 117, 137
  See also: Distributed system.

Index

Corporate data model 13, 17, 43, 45, 47
  corporate entities 33
  corporate entity 34, 40
  See also: Logical data modelling.
Correspondence 31, 32, 117, 124, 125, 132, 133, 142, 143, 148
  one-to-one correspondence 31, 32, 142
Data 8, 11, 13, 15, 17-19, 24, 26-29, 31-33, 37, 40, 43-45, 47, 49, 56, 87, 90, 91, 93, 97, 98, 103, 109, 110, 115, 117-120, 123, 127-129, 132-134, 136, 137, 139, 142-146, 148
  data storage 11, 27, 115, 145
  stored data 11, 27, 145
Database 11, 15, 21-24, 32, 34, 38, 87, 101, 102, 108, 126, 129, 136, 137, 139, 143, 145, 147
  relational database 11, 147
Database management system 143
  DBMS 29, 101, 136, 143
Data Flow Model 120, 129, 143
  DFM 120, 121, 127-129, 143
  logical DFM 120, 129
Data modelling.
  See: Logical data modelling and Corporate data model.
Dialogue design 96, 119, 125
  dialogue 26, 87, 96-98, 117, 119, 125, 133, 134, 147
  'stubs' 93, 125
Distributed system 29, 95, 128, 130
  See also: Coordinated system.
Effect correspondence diagram 143
  ECD 78, 79, 81-85, 84, 86, 112, 124, 135, 142, 143
  ECD fragment 82-84
  fragmented ECD 79
Enquiry 14, 24, 27, 28, 34, 40, 43, 52-55, 56-58, 87, 89, 90, 94, 98, 101-104, 110, 115, 117, 120, 121, 125, 129, 133, 135-138, 142-147
  developing enquiry views 52
  enquiries on shared entities 56
  enquiries that span applications 54
  enquiry fragment 53-55
  enquiry trigger 65
  enquiry view 57
  extending general enquiries 57
  merging results of 94
  reusable enquiry fragment 54

Enquiry Access Path 143, 144
   EAP 24, 52, 143
Enquiry Process Model 144, 146
   additional operation type 125
   EPM 125, 144
   operations list 144, 146, 148
Entity 7-9, 11, 12, 14, 24, 25, 31, 33, 34, 37-40, 45-49, 56, 59, 62, 101-103, 106, 107, 112, 115, 117, 122-127, 129-131, 133, 136, 137, 140, 141, 143, 144, 146-148
   Entity aspect 40
Entity-event modelling 8, 37
   Entity-Event Matrix 45, 46, 129
   event 8, 14, 26-28, 34, 37, 40, 43, 45-47, 61, 78, 89, 90, 98, 102, 115, 120, 121, 124, 125, 129, 131, 135, 136, 138, 143, 144, 147-149
   event identification 129
   event processes spanning more than one application 70
   event processes within a single application 66
   identifying events 25
   super-event 148
   See also: entity life history analysis.
Entity Life History analysis 124
   developing entity life histories 59
   ELH 37, 59-63, 86, 108, 112, 124, 133, 141, 143, 146, 148
   Entity Life Histories 59, 133, 140, 148
   Entity Life History 11, 124, 143, 144
   parallel life 37, 62, 63, 108
   parallel life histories 62
   parallel lives 37, 38, 62, 141, 146
   See also: entity-event modelling.
Euromethod 118, 140, 142, 144
   BPV 142
   Business Process View 142
External design 10, 11, 13, 14, 29, 57, 89-91, 93-98, 110, 115, 117, 120, 122, 124, 132, 137, 141, 144
   external design of subsequent applications 95
   external design of the first application 89, 91
   inputs 11, 13, 15, 25-27, 43, 45, 98
   multiple external designs 29
   outputs 11-13, 24, 25, 27, 32, 43, 52, 97, 119, 131
External schema 27, 28, 144
   See also: External design.
Feasibility Study 44, 116, 118, 126-128, 139, 148

Index

Function 28-30, 36, 89, 90, 94, 95, 97, 103, 104, 117, 119-122, 125, 136, 137, 141, 143, 144
Graphical user interface
 menus 11, 29, 90
Implementation 14, 21, 28, 34, 36, 45, 50, 87, 112, 120, 136, 141, 142, 146
 3 schemata are implemented as code 11, 30
Incremental delivery 145
Information Management Library Volumes
 Corporate Data Modelling 8, 139
 Data Management 8, 139
Inheritance 39, 144
Integration 7, 9-12, 14, 15, 21, 43, 106, 109, 118, 128
 first-cut database design for 101
 integrating 123
 requirements in Feasibility Report 127
 separation of different entity behaviours 47
 technique modifications 116
 See also: Conceptual Model.
Internal design 10, 11, 13, 15, 29, 37, 101, 115, 141, 145
 design optimisation 101, 102, 137
 first-cut internal design 101
Internal schema 27, 29, 145
 See also: Internal Design.
Investigation of current environment 147
ISE Library Volumes 8, 10, 21, 29, 32, 44, 45, 47, 86, 101, 118, 124, 130, 135, 147, 148
 An Introduction to Reuse 8, 139
 Applying Soft Systems Methodology to an SSADM Feasibility Study 118, 126, 139, 148
 Customising SSADM 8, 10, 21, 147
 Distributed Systems: Application Development 8, 32, 47, 101, 135, 139
 Managing Reuse 8, 29, 139
 Reuse in SSADM using Object-Orientation 8, 32, 86, 124, 139, 148
IT System 11, 21, 23, 24, 26, 27, 44, 45, 89, 93, 120, 121, 141, 149
Logical data model 11, 13, 17, 18, 24, 31, 127, 129, 143, 145, 146
 LDM 17, 19, 24-27, 31-34, 37, 38, 43, 45, 47-52, 57, 58, 9, 87, 101, 105-107, 109-112, 115, 116, 119, 123, 126-129, 131, 135, 141, 142, 145
 Required System Logical Data Model 24

155

Logical data modelling 31, 32, 117, 123
  content of the LDM 24
  data modelling 8, 31, 32, 117, 123, 139
  data model partition 13
  division of LDM to support self-contained subsystems 4
  ECDs for LDM loops 74
  loops between applications 78
  relating model to business 26
  shared entity type 49
  subtype 40
  testing the LDM 24
  updating the LDM 24
  See also: Corporate data model.
Logical design 29, 36, 134, 135, 143, 146
Logical process models 125
  See also: Enquiry Process Model and Update Process Model.
Message 34
  consistent behaviour of objects in response 112
  message passing 146
  message traffic 101
  multiple messages for a single event hitting a record instance 138
Optimisation 94, 101, 102, 124, 133, 137
  optimise 50, 137
Parallel development 7
Parallel lives 37, 38, 62, 141, 146
Partitioning 7, 9-11, 13, 14, 21, 34, 40, 43, 44, 47, 63, 64, 89, 90, 105-107, 116, 118, 119, 121, 126, 127, 130, 145, 146
  partition 10, 13, 32, 34, 47, 98, 105, 112, 116, 126, 127, 145
  partitioned 13, 29, 37, 43, 49, 50, 85, 90, 101, 105, 109, 112, 115, 128, 137
  partition manager process 112
  See also: Application and Conceptual model.
Physical design 29, 32, 87, 103, 126, 135-138
PPM Library Volumes 127
  A Guide to Programme Management 8, 117, 127, 139
  An Introduction to Programme Management 8, 117, 139

Index

Process 13, 26, 27, 43, 83, 84, 87, 94, 98, 102-104, 110, 112, 113, 115, 117, 125, 129, 135, 137, 141, 142, 144-146, 148, 149
   process invocation 87
Process-data interface 146
   PDI 27, 101-103, 126, 137, 138, 145, 146
   program-data interface 15, 87
Programme 7, 8, 44, 117, 126, 127, 131, 134, 139
   projects in a programme 127, 131
   subprojects starting from a single project 128
Project partitioning 34, 89
Projects-R-Us 9, 11, 15, 17, 18, 22, 23, 26, 31, 33, 34, 36-40, 44-50, 52, 57, 62, 78, 79, 85, 91-95, 97-99, 101-104, 105, 106, 108, 109, 111
   project control 11, 12, 15, 16, 19, 32, 35, 36, 45, 47, 49, 51, 54, 56, 59, 63, 64, 81-84, 91, 92, 94, 97-99, 103, 104, 105, 106, 109, 110
   project control application 11, 12, 32, 51, 63, 64, 82, 83, 91, 92, 94, 103, 106, 109, 110
   time-recording 94, 104
   time-recording application 94
   training 11, 12, 15-17, 19, 25, 26, 28, 31, 32, 35, 36, 44, 45, 47-49, 51, 52, 54, 56, 57, 59, 61, 78, 79, 81, 84-87, 92-99, 102, 103, 105, 106, 108-111, 119
   training application 49, 51, 52, 84, 85, 92, 94, 103, 109, 110
Prototype 133
Real-world 10-12, 22, 23, 31, 33, 38, 40, 41, 40, 47, 141, 142
Relational Data Analysis 24, 123, 133, 148
   RDA 123
Relationship 38, 49, 51, 52, 78, 110, 112, 119, 146
Requirements Analysis 23, 147
Requirements Specification 132, 134
Scope 14, 23, 24, 27, 43, 51, 53, 109, 115, 119, 126-128, 132, 135, 143, 145, 147, 148
Separately-developed systems 7
Shared server 47-50, 53, 56, 59, 81, 82, 106, 123, 131
   merging with a primary application 50
   shared servers may be merged into applications 106, 107
Soft Systems Methodology 44, 118, 126, 139, 147, 148
SSADM 7-11, 15, 21, 23, 24, 27, 29, 30, 32, 44, 47, 62, 86, 115-127, 129-137, 139, 140, 141, 142, 146-148

SSADM contd.
  Rationale 21, 147
  structural model 10, 21, 115, 120, 121, 126
  V4 Reference Manuals 10, 116, 124, 127, 129,
    134, 136, 137, 140, 142
Subsystem 27, 34, 37, 39, 44, 89, 145
Technical System Options 134
Universal function model 29, 30, 141
Update Process Model 146, 148, 149
  additional operation type 125
  operations list 144, 146, 148
  reusable update processes 85
  UPM 78, 81-84, 112, 125, 148, 149
Updating 24, 28, 45
  update 14, 26, 27, 47, 85, 87, 95, 101-103, 123, 125, 126,
    135, 137, 142-146, 148, 149
  updated 34, 90
User job design 119
User role 29, 99, 122, 129, 131, 132, 149
Workstation 93, 94